FAMILY PRESERVATION

Family Preservation

An Orientation For Administrators & Practitioners

Elizabeth Cole, M.S.W.
Joy Duva, M.S.W.

Child Welfare League of America, Washington, DC
(with the support of ther Edna McConnell Clark Foundation)

CHILD WELFARE LEAGUE OF AMERICA, INC.
440 First Street, NW, Suite 310, Washington, DC 20001-2085

CURRENT PRINTING (last digit)
10 9 8 7 6 5 4 3 2

Cover design by Kevin Erskine
Text design by Eve Malakoff-Klein

Printed in the United States of America

ISBN #0–87868–404–2

Library of Congress Cataloging-in-Publication Data

Cole, Elizabeth.
    Family Preservation : an orientation for administrators and
    practitioners / by Elizabeth Cole and Joy Duva.
        p.   cm.
    ISBN 0–87868–404–2
    1. Family services--United States.   2. Family social work--United
States.   I. Duva, Joy.   II. Edna McConnell Clark Foundation.
III. Title.
HV699.C534   1990
362.82'53'0973--dc20   90–1990
                                                                 CIP

Contents

Acknowledgments

This handbook was made possible through the generosity of a grant from the Edna McConnell Clark Foundation to the Child Welfare League of America. It was developed in part as a result of the experience of a network of family preservation programs funded by the Edna McConnell Clark Foundation. We commend Peter Forsythe, Vice President of the Edna McConnell Clark Foundation, for his vision in supporting and promoting family preservation services. We are grateful to the following network members for having the courage to test these service principles and for lending their knowledge and experience to the conceptualization and development of this handbook:

Jill Kinney, Behavioral Sciences Institute, Federal Way, Washington

David Haapala, Behavioral Sciences Institute, Federal Way, Washington

Nonnie Wilson, Families First, Portland, Oregon

Foday Kamara, formerly of Centers for New Horizons, Chicago, Illinois

Frances Jackson, Centers for New Horizons, Chicago, Illinois

Carolyn Brown, Commonweal Family Counseling, San Rafael, California

Neil Scheiman, Commonweal Family Counseling, San Rafael, California

Wanda Brasgala, Home Education Livelihood Program, Albuquerque, New Mexico

Maudelle Davis, Kingsley House, New Orleans, Louisiana

Patricia Watson, Kingsley House, New Orleans, Louisiana

Peter Horner, North Carolina Child Mental Health Services of Vance, Granville, Franklin, and Warren Counties

Alex Fonvielle, North Carolina Child Mental Health Services of Vance, Granville, Franklin, and Warren Counties

Ann Raynolds, Beacon Counseling, Inc., Boston, Massachusetts

Norma Garcia, Beacon Counseling, Inc., Boston, Massachusetts

Gail Purdy, Youth Services, Inc., Philadelphia, Pennsylvania

Jane Kowarsky, formerly of Youth Services, Inc., Philadelphia, Pennsylvania

Ralph Cordes, Sweetser Children's Home, Saco, Maine

Barbara Heath, Sweetser Children's Home, Saco, Maine

We appreciate the many public agency staff members who shared their experiences and thoughts with us. We want to thank Patrick McCarthy, Ph.D., Division Director, Department of Services for Children, Youth, and Families, Wilmington, Delaware, for contributing the chapter on evaluation.

We are most appreciative of those who took the time to review and comment on the draft:

Carolyn Billingsley, Commission for Children and Youth, Landover, Maryland

Jeane Zamosky, Family Strength, Concord, New Hampshire

Ying-Ying Yuan, Walter McDonald Associates, Sacramento, California

Cecelia Sudia, Children's Bureau, Department of Health and Human Services, Washington, DC

Special thanks to the following individuals: Sarah Greenblat, who compiled information on the agencies; Nancy Toland (CWLA), who typed the manuscript; Christine Hiley (CWLA), who revised the manuscript; Carl Schoenberg (CWLA), who edited the manuscript; and Joyce Strom, Deputy Director (CWLA), for her continuing support.

Introduction

The Adoption Assistance and Child Welfare Act of 1980 mandates child welfare agencies to make "reasonable efforts" to prevent the placement of children in foster care. Family preservation services represent one type of service model that agencies have begun to incorporate into their continuum of family and children's services to meet this requirement. This handbook was written for administrators, practitioners, child advocates, and policymakers as an introduction to the concepts, philosophy, nature, and scope of family preservation services. It describes what is unique, dynamic, and effective about this approach to working with families.

Stimulating interest in developing family preservation services and offering preliminary guidance in the initial planning efforts are the handbook's major purposes. It provides an overview of how and why the service works, identifies decision points in program development, and offers advantages, disadvantages, and considerations for various choices in program design. It raises the issues and questions that must be thought through in the planning process. The references cited throughout are an added source of information on various aspects of family preservation services, but most of the program and practice characteristics detailed in this book were elicited in interviews with voluntary and public agency staff members in family preservation services.

In thus summarizing the experience of those who are managing and delivering family preservation services, the book should be considered a work in progress. Family preservation services are still in an early stage of development, with much yet to be learned and done: further testing of family preservation services with various target populations; developing models of interagency collaboration; and designing interventions to deal effectively with substance abuse in families. This book, it is hoped, will advance the process of developing and expanding family preservation services across the country.

1

Definition and Program Characteristics

Definition

W hat are family preservation services? When and why are such services used?

Until recently, the term family preservation services could include literally anything done by a human services agency to help a family. It is now more commonly used to describe a unique and powerful set of interventions at the point of a family crisis that is likely to result in the imminent removal of a child from the home. (Family preservation services are sometimes referred to by a variety of terms, including intensive family services, intensive home-based services, and intensive family-centered crisis intervention services.)

Not necessarily the first line of defense, family preservation services are often employed only after all other assistance has failed, or has been judged inappropriate.

Family preservation services have three goals:

To keep the family safe

To avoid unnecessary placement of children in substitute care and the consequent high human and fiscal cost

To improve family functioning so that the behavior that led to the crisis will be less likely to occur

They are not just any services, but a distinctive form of family assistance with characteristics that vary dramatically from those

1

ordinarily available now and in the past. At their core is a deeply embedded set of values about families and the nature of help to them. These beliefs shape and sustain the programs. The synergism of values and characteristics results in a powerful and effective service.

Program Characteristics

Immediate Response to Referrals

Unlike other services that may take days, weeks, or months to respond, family preservation service makes contact with the family, for several important reasons, within 24 hours: (1) the crisis itself needs immediate attention; (2) when family breakup or child safety is an issue, it must be dealt with immediately; and (3) the crisis offers a unique opportunity for growth. Family members know that change is imperative and are more open to new ways of perceiving their problems and changing their behaviors.

Imminent Risk of Unnecessary Removal

Family preservation services are targeted on families in crisis: (1) those whose children are at the highest risk of placement; and (2) those whom the referral source believes family preservation services can help in such a way as to avert placement. The crisis may occur because of the escalation of problems, or because the family's ability to cope with problems has diminished. In either case, the crisis puts the children at imminent risk of placement outside of their home.

Assessment and Treatment Focus

The family as a unit and their relationship to the community in which they live constitute the focus of assessment and treatment.

A child's welfare is the paramount reason for an agency's intervening in a family's life. Charged with legal responsibility for protecting vulnerable children, agencies direct help to the children as individuals, frequently forgetting that their well-being depends on the well-being of their family. Families are viewed as a group of individuals, often assessed and treated as if they functioned in isolation from one another, rather than as a dynamic interacting unit in which every member influences and is influenced by the others.

Family preservation services are family focused, with the interaction among family members, and the associated behaviors, as the point for change. Shifts of behavior by any member alter the whole family in some way. An individual's problems affect the whole family. Progress of individual family members can be simultaneous on different parts of a problem, but always the whole family is the focus of assessment and treatment.

Families are also viewed and treated as part of a larger community that can weaken or support them. Effective family preservation services use and work with the social environment and explore a variety of formal and informal supports.

Limited Treatment Objectives

Objectives for family members are specific and measurable, not vague and general. They are determined by clients in consultation with the worker, not unilaterally conceived by the worker and announced to the family. Objectives target those problems and behaviors that precipitated the placement crisis, not all the family's problems. The central objective of family preservation services is to help the family get through this crisis without separation of the child, and in the process learn new skills that will help them to solve future problems. For many families this intervention begins a growth process that continues long after the service ends. The skills taught and the insights gained during the course of treatment strengthen the family's ability to cope with stress after the crisis is past. Some families may not want or need more help once the services are terminated. Others will need additional formal or informal support.

Although providers of family preservation may be instrumental in helping the family develop a long-term plan for services and continued change, they do not deliver long-term assistance themselves.

The Clients' Home and Community as the Locus of All Services

Family preservation services are premised on a philosophy about the locus of service radically different from tradition: it should be delivered where the family lives. This does not mean making occasional home visits to supplement the office-based therapy, or going to the home only long enough to bring about the willingness and ability of clients to keep office appointments. It denotes that almost all time spent with the clients will be spent in their home and community.

There are several important philosophical and therapeutic reasons why this should be so. Serving families in their homes embraces the notion that the agency serves the family, but the family controls its own destiny. Office visits serve the convenience of agency staff members, thus conveying the notion that the helper is in a superior and more powerful position.

Providing services in a home acknowledges that the unique reality of each family is best grasped and dealt with within its own environment. Spending time in the family's home provides sharper and quicker insights into how a family really functions than office-based interviews can do. Individuals are not good informants about how they actually behave. They may honestly think of themselves as good listeners, reasonable negotiators, and firm disciplinarians, but the reality may be far different. In an office visit clients report how they behave. In their homes they can be seen behaving. Just as the best account of another country is no substitute for living there awhile, observing family boundaries, identifying roles and values, knowing who belongs to a particular family, who are its friends and its enemies, and what emotional climate prevails, can be done best only in the family's home and environment. Teaching opportunities abound at home. New behaviors can be modeled or discussed immediately after negative experiences with old behavior patterns. The safety of family members is also best monitored by a practitioner who spends more time with the family than in the office.

Some practitioner-family contacts do occur outside the home. Practitioners may accompany and bolster family members who visit other helpers: schools, courts, doctors, public assistance offices. Time is spent in activities that support family members and encourage self-esteem and a sense of well-being.

The Range of Services

Family preservation services offer a mix of counseling, education, information and referral, concrete assistance, and advocacy.

Every family presents a different assortment of needs, desires, and resources. Some existing services often meet every family with the same limited response. Counseling is the most common remedy offered. Clearly, discussion and teaching are necessary ingredients in helping families, but most poor families put filling other basic needs as their priority. They will not, cannot, and should not be asked to participate in discussions of relationships when their consuming preoccupation is food, warmth, shelter, or medical care—the concrete services.

Providing or brokering concrete services are key components of family preservation services. It is often in joint pursuit of these services that worker and family gain trust, and teachable moments and true counseling occur. Once the family members experience concrete help, they are more trusting that other forms of assistance are possible.

Advocating for clients is part of the family preservation practitioner's job description. Sometimes the practitioner will intervene with other helping organizations on behalf of the clients, although teaching families how to advocate for themselves is the first course of action. There is a larger and more difficult advocacy role, however—taking action to better the environmental circumstances that create or contribute to the family problems. Advocating for more affordable housing for low-income families or for improvement in the schools in poor neighborhoods illustrates this larger advocacy role.

Availability of Services

Crises are unpredictable, by definition. They aren't all scheduled between nine and five, Monday through Friday, nor is it possible for all family members to be home during these hours. Service must be available when it is needed or at times when it will be effective. Incidents occurring in the evenings or on weekends may provide the best teaching occasions or opportunities for insight into family functioning. It is important that families be able to reach their practitioner immediately when a crisis occurs. Practitioners frequently give families their own and their supervisor's home telephone numbers, rather than depend on the agency operators or the emergency phone staff to refer calls.

Intensive Intervention

The time devoted to contacts in a family's home ranges from five to 20 hours a week. Longer periods may be spent at the beginning of service to defuse high emotions, understand problems and family dynamics, obtain desperately needed material assistance, and so forth. Intensity and flexibility are crucial to the monitoring required to assure the safety of family members. The number of direct service hours with the family decreases as the family achieves its goals and increases its ability to resolve problems.

Short-Term Intervention

Models with a single practitioner working with one or two families generally use a four to six-week time frame. Models that employ a team approach with a slightly higher caseload may extend the time frame to 12 weeks. Time limits are made clear to the family from the outset. Stipulating an end to service compels family members and practitioners alike to focus on solving problems and on constantly monitoring progress. Knowing that it will not last longer than six or 12 weeks makes the intensity of the contacts and the relentless pressure to attain goals tolerable for both family and staff members.

Caseload Size

The requirements of intensity, flexibility, and brevity preclude a caseload larger than two or three families at any one time for a single practitioner. Two families is the optimal caseload size. Models that use a team approach have more service hours available and therefore may have a slightly larger caseload—up to six families. Families are phased into a caseload. As new cases that require more intensive work are added, others are phased out and require less service. Because cases terminate within four to 12 weeks, family preservation practitioners or teams are able to serve up to 24 families a year. Services to families are "sequential" (two or three families served at a time) rather than "simultaneous" (serving 24 families for a whole year or more). As a result, the yearly number of sequential cases is comparable to simultaneous caseloads, but there is one striking difference. The record of efficiency, goal attainment, and practitioner and client satisfaction is measurably better with small caseloads.

Values and Assumptions Underlying the Program

Values and assumptions mold and shape the delivery of services as thoughts mold actions. One cannot understand or implement effective family preservation services without examining the beliefs that underpin them. They fall into two broad organizing categories:

beliefs about the nature and importance of families, and beliefs about the nature of help to families.

There are at least three main themes around which the extenuated beliefs regarding families and society seem to cluster: the privacy of the family; the need for limited intervention by the state and its helping organizations; and the responsibility of the state to protect the due process rights of families. As a society we say we believe that all human beings—and children in particular—need to be attached to and nurtured by other human beings. We further say we believe that in children these needs are best met when children are raised in families where they can be protected, sheltered, socialized, and helped to become adults who will contribute to the society.

When individuals are in trouble they often reach out to parents and/or siblings. Many families in the community, particularly poor families, have no one who is willing or able to help. To respond to them, the community has created social agencies to substitute for extended family members and friends. The governing principles binding the organizations that support the privacy of the family are these:

> Most children should live in legally recognized permanent families.

> It is the helping organization's task to preserve the family of origin whenever feasible and to provide another permanent family when it is not.

> Failing this, children should be provided with continuity in relationships with nurturing caregivers.

Unfortunately, these principles are often ignored:

> Young neglected children are removed instead of their mother being provided with needed supports.

> Family members or friends are not explored or are devalued as sources of help.

> Runaway adolescents have their flight abetted and supported by practitioners rather than halted by a plan to remain at home and work on problems.

> Because it is easier on the family and the school, many emotionally disturbed children are placed in some form of care rather than treated in the community.

Community members generally feel the same discomfort with severely disabled families that they do with severely disabled individuals. They really don't want to look at them and prefer that someone else take care of them and at some distance.

The right of the family to privacy dictates that agencies practice limited intervention and protect their clients' due process rights. It is fundamental to the American belief in freedom that there should be only carefully limited intervention into families by the state and its helping organizations. Generally, families are entitled to raise children as they think best, so long as they conform to the laws and norms of our society. The state and its agencies may interfere in the life of the family only with serious justification. The state's intervention should not exceed that which is needed to rectify the cause for intervention.

This principle applies characteristically to family preservation services. The service notion of limited objectives is congruent with limited intervention. Once the problems for which an agency was called in have been resolved, the service should end. Work on other issues should continue only if the family wants to be helped with them. Family preservation services do not pretend to cure all family ills, nor are there illusions that there will never be another crisis. The family's need for a social agency's help is clearly seen as episodic rather than continuous.

Helpers must also be sure to protect the due process rights of clients—both parents and children. Translated into social service parlance, this legal concept means that practitioners must conscientiously inform families of their rights and responsibilities, their role in forming the service plan, the consequences of their failure to perform according to plan, their right to representation, and the process to be followed if there is a disagreement.

Certain clinical assumptions are consonant with these democratic beliefs about families, and in accord with the underlying principle of family empowerment and the avoidance of dependency. Clinical strategies should be aimed at developing the family's ability to help themselves. This is predicated on the value assumption that most troubled families can and want to eliminate their problems and can make changes. The pain, fear, and anger generated by a family crisis can produce enough energy to motivate a family to learn new patterns. Although the crisis is an opportunity, it also presents the potential danger that the helper will take control from sometimes all-too-willing family members. The practitioner may spend an enormous amount of time and involvement with the family, but the intent is to exercise as minimal an amount of control over family decisions as possible, consonant with maintaining the safety of the family members. Belief in the primacy and power of families is the basic rationale for working with the family as a whole and delivering the services in the family's home.

Family Preservation and the Gateways to Out-of-Home Placement

The primary goal of family preservation services is the prevention of unnecessary placement of children outside their families. It stands to reason, then, that these services should be located at the organizational gateways where children are separated from their parents. These are generally within the traditional service systems: child welfare, juvenile justice, mental health, and developmental disabilities. All too frequently, initiatives are lodged only within one helping system and are not connected to or coordinated among agencies or among departments. This is a serious problem. A family with the same set of problems may be preserved or have its children placed depending on which community organization it applies to or is referred to. Yet there are logical places within each placing agency or organizational process where referral to family preservation services is possible.

At present, all of the placement systems have fairly similar methods for handling family cases. First, there is a process for case opening. In some systems there may be legal complaints, in others simply referrals for service. Second, some form of assessment, investigation, or diagnosis takes place. Third, a decision is made on the disposition of the case. Several are possible: (1) do nothing and dismiss the case; (2) apply community help, that is, services to children in their own homes—probation, community mental health, or rehabilitation services; or (3) separate children from the family by placing them in a foster family or group care.

Family preservation services fit between option two and three, and add a fourth option appropriate for those cases where less intensive interventions will not do and separation is an imminent risk. The end product of the family preservation services intervention may be to close the case for no further action, refer the family for less intensive community-based services, or refer the child for an out-of-home placement.

Family preservation services can enhance the efficacy of placement services for those families in which placement is deemed necessary:

> Family preservation services raise the quality of, and confidence in, the validity of the placement decision, and meet the requirement that all reasonable efforts have been made to prevent placement.

> More intimate knowledge of the child and family may lead to a more appropriate choice of placement and a better plan for, and possibility of, family involvement.

> A positive family involvement may hasten the child's reunification with his or her family.

> If placement is recommended because there is little hope of family rehabilitation, the documented evidence based on an intensive effort could lead to earlier action to terminate parental rights, or other permanency plans. Greater knowledge of the child's ability to function in a family will facilitate decisions on adoptive recruitment, placement, and postplacement services.

Family preservation services were conceived and are primarily used to prevent unnecessary placements into substitute care. They can also be used to maintain stability and continuity, however, for children living in foster families, group care, or adoptive families. The need for the service among these agency-created families is growing because of the increased severity of children's problems and the shortage of substitute parents.

Services may be delivered by public or private agencies. The appropriate choice for any given jurisdiction depends on a number of factors that are discussed in Chapter 4.

2

History

The debate over service to troubled families began long before our current efforts to reform children's services in mental health, child welfare, and juvenile justice. American communities have struggled with the same set of problems since the communities were established. What do you do with malfunctioning parents—punish them, ignore them, or help them? What authority does the community have to intervene in the lives of troubled families? What should be the nature of the intervention? Although the questions and problems today and in the past may be alike, each age finds answers that reflect its values, technology, and resources. As major changes occur in any or all of these areas, so too do the solutions change.

Sometimes, however, the current remedies are not entirely new. They may have been suggested and tried before and are being reemphasized. New technology may be used to implement old principles. Family preservation services embrace a collection of long-held and mostly ignored values, some new techniques, and some old techniques that are being reemphasized. The beliefs discussed in the first chapter are recast in the language of current technology and advocated with a renewed sense of urgency.

Child welfare in America began as an effort to rescue and save children who were being hurt, neglected, or abandoned by their parents. Agencies stepped in when problems were serious. The responsibility of caring for these children overshadowed child welfare's attempts to mend their families or to intervene earlier when problems were just starting. This pattern was to carry into the twentieth century, where this history begins.

11

Early Roots of Family Preservation

In 1909, Theodore Roosevelt convened the first White House Conference on Dependent Children so that those engaged in the work of caring for dependent and destitute children could exchange ideas and experiences. The discussion was wide-ranging and resulted in 13 recommendations to the president; one had to do with efforts to keep families together.

The conference set forth the principle that home life is the highest and finest product of civilization. It is the great molding force of mind and of character. Children should not be deprived of it except for urgent and compelling reasons. Children of parents of "worthy character," who are suffering from temporary misfortune, and children of reasonably efficient and "deserving" mothers who are without the support of the normal breadwinner, should as a rule be kept with their parents, with such aid being given as may be necessary to maintain suitable homes for the rearing of the children. Aid should be given by such methods and from such sources as may be determined by the general relief policy of each community, preferably in the form of private charity rather than of public relief. Except in unusual circumstances, the home should not be broken up for reasons of poverty, but only for considerations of inefficiency or "immorality." With few exceptions, most delegates agreed that "workers in the field of charity make extraordinary efforts to preserve the family" [Bremner 1971].

After the conference, financial aid legislation authorizing "mother's pensions" was passed in many states. This assistance preserved the home and prevented placement for a substantial number of children [McGowan 1988]. The concept of mother's pensions took hold and was transformed into the Aid to Dependent Children provisions of the Social Security Act of 1935.

Not every family was considered worthy of a mother's pension or any other form of help. "Immoral" mothers and those of "bad character" were often barred from assistance. Furthermore, the concept of the mother's pension was based on the simplistic notion that the majority of children were placed because their parents didn't have enough money. This view ignored the other incapacities of parents or the challenges to parenting that some children presented [Bremner 1971]. Foster care therefore expanded together with Aid to Dependent Children.

Most of the time and effort of child welfare workers went into the maintenance of children in foster care. In the 1940s some authors in the field denied that agencies lacked involvement with the parents of children in care or about to enter care [Hutchinson 1944; Gordon 1941]. Other writers began to question openly whether all children benefit from foster care.

> One has only to have made a few close observations of some of the problems connected with boarding home care to know that there have been times when every experienced and thinking child welfare worker has been tormented by some doubts as to the efficacy of this method of caring for dependent and neglected children. In fact, there are occasions when a worker viewing the end result of long years of foster care for a particular child will remark with both candor and discouragement that the child could not have been much worse off if he had remained in his own home. [Jolowicz 1946]

Growing Momentum in Mid-Century

It was not until 1959 that a large-scale CWLA national study of foster care was to yield research data that confirmed certain weaknesses of the foster care system. Maas and Engler [1959] found that foster children had biological parents who seldom visited and seemed not to have plans for their return. The agencies that served the children also had vague and indefinite plans for the children's future. Two-thirds of the children were growing up in what was originally planned as a temporary foster home.

Following this study, CWLA called for the consideration of adoption for the children who would not be returning home from foster care [Shapiro 1959]. The CWLA director of standards urged the development of home-based services that would eliminate the need for many of the placements. She said, with some feeling:

> We cannot substitute platitudes about strengthening family life, preventing delinquency or promoting mental health for action. It is not enough to utter pious sentiments about our obligation to maintain children in their own homes, if those serve only to ease our conscience and relieve us of responsibility to do anything further. [Turitz 1961]

The lack of services was even more frustrating, because at that same time there was some programmatic evidence that intensive services to multiproblem families did help them. The St. Paul (Minnesota) Family-Centered Project, begun in the 1950s, yielded dramatic improvements among the most troubled families in the community—65% of the families made considerable gains. The families had been referred to the project because of serious neglect and/or juvenile delinquency [Birt 1956].

The project attributed its success with the families to certain key approaches and beliefs. (Coincidentally, these are nearly the same as the program attributes outlined in the first chapter.)

> Direct and unrelenting outreach to families, even when they were not asking for help, and even when they actively resisted professional intervention
>
> Steadfast conviction and optimism that even the most troubled and chaotic families can make positive changes
>
> Frank and completely aboveboard communication with the families, including the sharing of agency records and reports
>
> Most attention to the needs of the parents rather than to those of the children, even when the children were being neglected
>
> A focus on what the family wanted, not on what the worker, agency, or community wanted for the family
>
> Building a working relationship by demonstrating to the family that the practitioner could be of use to them in practical and tangible ways
>
> Extensive use of home visits, family interviews, and extraordinary efforts to involve the fathers
>
> Designation of one professional person as the coordinator of all services received by a family, even when the many services were coming from a variety of different agencies [Horejsi et al. 1981]

Following the St. Paul project in the 1950s, Maas and Engler's research in 1959, and Turitz's plan for family preservation services, the AFDC program and foster care programs expanded. But as McGowan [1988] points out:

Despite these federal initiatives, continued state expansion and regulation of service, and increased professionalization of staff, no systematic efforts were made until the past two decades to implement the concept of family preservation introduced at the first White House Conference on Children.

Impetus for the development of family preservation services in the 1970s and 1980s came from a number of sources.

Factors Influencing the Development and Expansion of Family Preservation Services

Growing Body of Research

During the 1970s the earlier findings of Maas and Engler regarding the long-term nature of foster care were confirmed by several researchers [Fanshel 1971; Fanshel and Shinn 1978; Gruber 1978; Wiltse and Gambrill 1974]. Each study urged a reappraisal and restructuring of child welfare to include family preservation, reunification, and adoption services.

Successful Program Models

During the early 1970s several agencies began, as the St. Paul project did, to deliver intensive services to families in care as a way of strengthening them by averting unnecessary placement. For example:

Homebuilders in Washington State is one such program. Begun in 1974, its goal was to strengthen families and thereby provide an alternative to hospitalization, incarceration, institutionalization, or foster care. Its initial research indicated that "96 percent of these families stay together until their crisis is passed and 86 percent are still together one year after intake." [Haapala and Kinney 1979]

In Minnesota, the Mendota Mental Health Institute initiated a Home and Community Treatment Program that demonstrated that intensive family intervention and education in parenting skills constituted an effective treatment for seriously emotionally disturbed children.

Increased Number of Children in Foster Care

In 1961 there were 177,000 children in foster care. By 1978 that figure had grown to 503,000 [Shyne and Schroeder 1978: 33]. These numbers kindled child advocates' concern about the well-being of the children. They also sparked the interest of a Congress intent on reducing federal spending on social programs. In 1975, then Secretary of Health, Education, and Welfare Casper Weinberger wrote to Senator Walter Mondale that there were an estimated 360,000 children in foster care for whom the federal expenditure alone was $31,055,000 in Title IV-B, Child Welfare Services; and $91,445,000 in Title IV-A, AFDC Foster Care Income Maintenance. The state and local contribution to foster care was more than double this amount [Subcommittee on Children and Youth 1975].

Federal Legislation

During the 1970s a number of federal laws were passed that were to redirect and initiate services to children and their families and to increase the number of families to be helped.

The Child Abuse Prevention and Treatment Act of 1974 required statewide systems of reporting and investigating child abuse and neglect complaints, thereby dramatically increasing the cases coming to the attention of child welfare agencies.

The Juvenile Justice and Delinquency Prevention Act of 1974, in addition to encouraging improvements in juvenile justice systems, also stimulated experiments in alternatives to incarceration.

The federal legislation that had the most bearing on the creation of family preservation services, however, was Public Law 96-272: The Adoption Assistance and Child Welfare Act of 1980. To be eligible for federal money, states were required to have a plan by October 1, 1983 that provided that *reasonable efforts* must in each case be made to prevent or eliminate the need for removal of children from their homes or to make it possible for them to return home. Family preservation services are or should be an essential component of each state's plan to satisfy the reasonable efforts requirement.

In addition to federal legislation, states have passed statutes enabling and encouraging family preservation services.

Other Federal Initiatives

In the mid-1970s the Children's Bureau of the Office of Human Development began to stimulate the creation of services, targeting grants for the development of models of home-based services, and focusing Section 426 training grant priorities on the reduction of family breakdown and the provision of supportive and preventive services.

The creation of a National Clearinghouse for Home-Based Services to Children, located at the University of Iowa (now The National Resource Center on Family-Based Services) was a major initiative.

Role of the Child Welfare League of America

Permanency planning has been a major concentration of CWLA for the last decade. The North American Center on Adoption established adoption as a viable option for minority children and those with special needs. The Permanent Families for Children Program promoted and achieved vital foster care reforms.

In 1987, CWLA received a two-year grant from the Edna McConnell Clark Foundation to conduct a range of public policy, advocacy, and technical assistance activities to promote the development and expansion of family preservation services, comprising the following:

Support and assist a network of family preservation agencies

Conceptualize the service in a handbook for practitioners and administrators

Endorse this service by incorporating it into CWLA standards and encouraging the Council on Accreditation to add it to its provisions

Educate the general public in conferences, speeches, and publications

Monitor public policy initiatives that ensure continuance of federal resources through appropriate titles of the Social Security Act

Link with other national organizations to assure their continued support and promotion of this agenda to preserve families

Provide training and consultation to public and private child welfare agencies

CWLA's experience with the family preservation network of agencies was a valuable source of information and knowledge about family preservation practice and the virtues and limitations of certain client approaches and organizational designs. The network helped clarify the values underpinning the programs and how to translate these values into practice. Most of what was learned is incorporated in this book. A description of the network agencies is in Appendix A.

Other Voluntary Organization Initiatives

In conjunction with the federal initiatives and those of CWLA, other national organizations have launched projects to inform their constituents about family preservation services and to develop strategies to ensure their implementation nationwide. They include: American Bar Association; American Public Welfare Association; Center for the Study of Social Policy; Children's Defense Fund; Florida Mental Health Institute; National Association of Foster Care Reviewers; National Child Welfare Leadership Center; National Conference of State Legislatures; National Council of Juvenile and Family Court Judges; and Youth Law Center.

Appendix B lists addresses and phone numbers for these organizations .

State Initiatives

The most powerful determinant of whether these services will be given ultimately lies with the nation's public child welfare agencies. Interest in delivering these services themselves or purchasing them from voluntary agencies is growing. Many states are establishing pilot family preservation programs; some are already implementing a plan for phasing in such services statewide. Currently, a network of state-level public child welfare agency representatives convened by CWLA meets regularly to exchange information and provide support and assistance in developing family preservation services.

Conclusion

We are at a critical juncture in the long history of our failure to provide truly useful services to strengthen family life and avoid unnecessary placement. The critical challenge to the field is to design and deliver the services in such a way that they will be as substantial and powerful as we know they can be. Otherwise they become an illusion of service—a fraud perpetrated on the children and families and on the community that authorizes and supports such services.

References

Birt, C. "The Family-Centered Project of St. Paul." *Social Work* 1(1956): 41–47.

Bremner, R.H. *Children and Youth in America: A Documentary History. Volume II: 1866–1932.* Parts 1–6. Cambridge, MA: Harvard University Press, 1971.

Fanshel, D. "The Exit of Children from Foster Care: An Interim Research Report." *Child Welfare* L, 2 (February 1971): 65–81.

Fanshel, D., and Shinn, E.B. *Children in Foster Care: A Longitudinal Investigation.* New York: Columbia University Press, 1978.

Gordon, H.L. "Discharge: An Integral Aspect of the Placement Process." *The Family* 22, 2 (March 1941): 35–42.

Gruber, N.R. *Children in Foster Care.* New York: Human Sciences Press, 1978.

Haapala D., and Kinney J. "Homebuilders' Approach to the Training of In-Home Therapists." In *Home-Based Services for Children and Families: Policies, Practice, and Research,* ed. Sheila Maybanks and Marvin Bryce. Springfield, IL: Charles C. Thomas, 1979, 248–259.

Horejsi, C.R.; Bertsche, A.V.; and Clark, F.W. *Social Work Practice with Parents of Children in Foster Care.* Springfield, IL: Charles C. Thomas, 1981.

Hutchinson, D. "The Request for Placement Has Meaning." *The Family* 25, 4 (June 1944): 128–132.

Jolowicz, A. "The Hidden Parent." In *Proceedings of the New York State Conference on Social Welfare.* New York: New York Department of Social Services, 1946, 1.

Maas, Henry, and Engler, Richard. *Children in Need of Parents.* New York: Columbia University Press, 1959.

McGowan, B.G. "Family-Based Services and Public Policy: Context and Implications."

In *Improving Practice Technology for Work with High Risk Families,* ed. J. Whittaker, J. Kinney, E.M. Tracey, and C. Booth. Seattle, WA: University of Washington, 1988.

Shapiro, M. A *Study of Adoption Practice.* New York: Child Welfare League of America, 1959.

Shyne, A.W., and Schroeder, A.G. *National Study of Social Services to Children and Their Families.* Washington, DC: U.S. Department of Health, Education, and Welfare, Publication Number OHD78-30150, 1978.

Subcommittee on Children and Youth. Committee on Labor and Public Welfare, United States Senate, 94th Congress. *Examination and Exploration of Existing and Proposed Federal Policies Affecting the Adoption of Children and Their Placement in the Foster Care System.* July 14–18, 1975.

Turitz, Z. "Obstacles to Services for Children in Their Own Homes." *Child Welfare* XL, 6 (June 1961): 1–6.

Wiltse, K.T., and Gambrill, E.D. "Foster Care: Plans and Actualities." *Public Welfare* 32, 2 (Spring 1974): 7–14.

3

Practice Considerations

I t is in the best interest of the child to work with the family unit to help parents resolve problems that are putting the child at risk of placement. Family preservation services offer families an opportunity to receive assistance in meeting their own goals for bettering their lives as individuals and as a family. As discussed earlier, to be a practitioner in family preservation services means embracing a set of values about families and becoming a facilitator for change rather than an authority figure.

The role of the family preservation practitioner may be thought of as similar to that of a consultant. To fulfill this role, the practitioner needs the ability or competency to:

Identify a problem

Make an analysis of the problems or issues and to interpret the results for the client

Communicate effectively with all types of client systems

Help other people become comfortable with change

Deal with conflict and confrontation

Develop objectives with the client

Help other people learn how to learn

Manage a development and growth effort

Evaluate results

Be creative and innovative in working with the client

Be self-renewing [Lippitt and Lippitt 1978]

The safety of the child is the primary concern of the family preservation practitioner, who must be skilled in assessing the risks of the child's staying in or being removed from a family, and taking action based on that assessment. The practitioner must be able to respond to situational emergencies that place a child at risk, as well as work with families planfully to reduce or eliminate chronic risk factors.

In discussing the beginning, middle, and ending phases of working with families in a family preservation service, it is important to remember that in most real situations the phases and tasks are not sequential but often simultaneous, and at their best, synergistic. The family and the practitioner are working together under the pressure of a specified time frame to accomplish certain goals. This chapter describes the various aspects of family preservation practice that together create the context for change to take place.

Beginning Phase

Eligibility Considerations

When cases are first referred to a family preservation service, information is generally screened to determine if family preservation services are potentially appropriate. After a practitioner sees the family face-to-face and assesses the family's situation, whether or not to accept the case for family preservation services can be decided.

The following are examples of case selection criteria:

1. *Criteria for acceptance.*

The child is at imminent risk of placement.

The child was recently removed from home (two to three weeks) and imminent return is expected.

The family members are committed to working together to solve problems and remain intact.

2. *Criteria for rejection.*

There is no imminent risk of placement.

Less intensive service is appropriate but has not yet been tried.

Homelessness is the only presenting problem and can be handled by a housing service.

The safety of the child cannot be assured.

The referral source will frequently know of several severe family problems that may or may not be a bar to service. The family preservation practitioner will have to make his or her own assessment of these conditions. For example, caregivers may be mentally ill or retarded, or abusing alcohol or other drugs. The assessment issue here is whether these conditions prohibit the individual from engaging in and benefiting from the proffered help, and whether the child will be safe in the home while treatment is continuing. Family preservation services differ from many traditional services, looking beyond labels to identify the family's strengths and capabilities.

The First Home Visit

Engagement. After an initial screening determines that family preservation services are potentially appropriate for the family, contact is generally made within 24 hours to schedule a home visit. If necessary, a home visit can be made within an hour. The process of engagement begins with this first call or contact. The practitioner's manner, tone of voice and willingness to schedule in relation to the family's circumstances helps create a positive beginning.

Engaging the family means developing a trusting relationship through which the family can establish and achieve its own goals. The first home visit is crucial to engaging the family. It sets the tone for the way that the family will be treated if it chooses to accept the service. The practitioner conveys his or her attitudes and values about families both directly and subtly. Selecting a time for the meeting that is convenient for the family and meeting on the family's turf are indirect ways of showing respect for the family. Politeness such as asking to enter the home or asking to be seated acknowledge that the practitioner is a guest in the family's home and respectful of their authority [Hartman 1983]. The most important initial goal is connecting with the family. Sometimes this occurs in the first few minutes or it may take several hours or days. A family's previous experience with helping professionals will often influence the family's initial response to the family preservation practitioner.

Of the many techniques the practitioner can use to break the ice and begin to engage the family, the most important is to be sincere and genuine and simply relate as one human being to another. Active listening, asking open-ended questions, establishing eye contact (note, though, that depending on the cultural context of the family, eye contact may not always be appropriate) are also important in engaging clients. In beginning conversation, the practitioner looks for neutral things to comment on to reduce the stress of the first meeting. For example, in visiting a rural family in a remote place, the practitioner might comment on the drive out to the home. Complimenting the children is a way to acknowledge the parents' care and concern for their children. A sincere compliment about the family or its environment helps to establish rapport and subtly tells the family members they are not being judged negatively. On the contrary, their achievements and accomplishments are being recognized.

On the one hand, a part of the engagement process is an acknowledgment that the client has more information about the family than the worker—the client is the "expert." On the other hand, client families lack certain skills, information, or resources to resolve their problems and make necessary changes; the practitioner brings a positive attitude and instills hope for the families that they can improve their current situation.

Some families may be hostile at first because previous experiences with the helping professions were not considered helpful. The practitioner, while letting the client ventilate angry feelings, empathizes and tries to find some common areas of agreement, emphasizing that the goal of family preservation services is to offer help and support to keep the family together. Simply showing understanding of the family's past experiences, their current situation, their pain, and their strengths, effectively brings family and practitioner together.

Although most social work involves engaging the client, the process is experienced somewhat differently by clients of family preservation services. First of all, the service takes place in their own home at times that are convenient to them. The whole family might be present, including extended family members and family friends. Long periods of time may be needed to give support to the family and help them to work through a problem. The practitioner stays as long as necessary and may be in the home for a whole day, if needed. Emergency needs can be met immediately; service is available 24 hours a day. The program is designed to facilitate engaging the family members by showing respect for their time, their strengths, and their ability to make changes that will improve their life as a family.

Problem/Strength Identification. The initial home visit usually takes two to three hours. During that time the practitioner decides whether the child can safely remain in the home and identifies any problems requiring immediate help, such as lack of food or heat.

The practitioner looks for strengths and competencies, as well as problems. Understanding individual competencies, positive relationships among family members, and positive ways the family functions as a unit is important to the helper. These strengths are the building blocks for future changes.

1. *Assessing child safety.*

If a case involves suspected child abuse or neglect, a protective services investigation would usually take place before the case is referred to family preservation services; referral means that although the child is at risk of placement, the protective services staff believes that immediate intensive work with the family can reduce significantly or eliminate the risk. Family preservation staff members, during the initial visit, must reassess whether the child can remain safely in the home. Circumstances may have changed since the protective services worker saw the family that could affect the child's safety.

Assessment tools are now available for evaluating risk to children remaining in their homes. A range of factors are examined and usually are weighted in some way to indicate low, medium, or high risk. They include the child's age, severity and frequency of abuse or neglect, location of injury, previous history of abuse or neglect, stresses, caregivers' cooperation, caregivers' intellectual and emotional abilities, and the family support system. Other factors contributing to the risk assessment include the immediacy of the risk of maltreatment, its controllability, and its likely recurrence.

The assessment should determine whether family preservation services can significantly reduce or eliminate risk to the child and how this can be accomplished. For example, in a situation where a new mother lacks parenting skills to care for a newborn, the family preservation worker might develop a plan with the mother involving the services of a parent aide during the day to teach and role-model parenting, as well as a relative who stays and helps the mother in the evening. Some situations, however, are too dangerous, and the children must be removed for their own safety. Consider, for example, the case of a family in which the father, an alcoholic who becomes violent when drunk, has physically abused his children. He refuses to go into treatment for his alcoholism. Although he will allow family preservation staff members into the home to talk with other family members, he refuses to become involved. If he will not participate in family preservation services or in an alcohol treatment program, the children are considered at high risk for abuse. A referral to protective services for placement is appropriate.

At the time of risk assessment, the practitioner should also consider the harmful psychological damage to the child that could result from a separation from the family. For example, what harm might be done by removing a two-week old child from its nursing mother?

2.   *Assessing basic needs.*

Families will be more open to working on problems in family functioning once their basic needs are met. The practitioner must identify concrete needs that, if not met, threaten the family's survival. Family preservation services develop linkages with churches and community organizations that offer transportation and emergency assistance for food, shelter, clothing, and furniture. It is a key component of an effective family preservation service to have discretionary funds to meet emergency needs when there are no other resources that can be used. By focusing on the concrete problems, the practitioner rapidly establishes a basis for trust. The family experiences tangible help with a critical problem. By responding immediately to the family's most pressing need, the practitioner demonstrates not only sensitivity and a desire to help, but also the capability to make a positive difference in the family's life. This is particularly important for families whose past involvements with service

agencies have made them skeptical that anyone can really
help them [Intensive Family Services 1987].

3.   General assessment.

Once emergency needs have been met, the practitioner
can focus on problem areas, as well as family strengths. By
interacting with family members and observing their interactions with each other, the practitioner assesses areas such
as communication patterns and skills, parenting abilities,
limit-setting, and the nature and quality of relationships
within the family.

The family's contacts with outside systems and supports are also of interest to the practitioner. What informal
supports—such as extended family, neighbors, friends, reli-
gious organizations—are available to provide various kinds
of assistance when the family needs help? Whether the
family knows about and is able to gain access to formal
community services such as health services, financial assistance, education, job training and employment services is
important information [Whittaker et al. 1989].

Because the practitioner works in the family home and
is with the family for frequent, concentrated periods of time,
he or she is able to gather a relatively comprehensive and
accurate picture of the family's life. Little can be hidden for
very long. Sometimes family secrets and problems surface
that have long existed but were undetected by other service
providers or during a protective services investigation. For
example, families often feel free to reveal hidden problems
such as sexual abuse or substance abuse.

Client families often feel incompetent, and previous
helpers have somehow reinforced their lack of self-esteem
and self-confidence. To counterbalance such past experiences and help the family members rebuild their sense of
worth, the practitioner points out and compliments them on
strengths and competencies and uses these in designing
strategies for achieving goals.

Practitioner and family are continually reassessing
progress toward goal achievement. New factors may occur

in the family's life at any time that may result in a change or modification of goals.

4. *Specialized assessment.*

Some family preservation programs also incorporate specialized types of assessments to ensure that possible physical causes of problem behaviors are identified. For example, Commonweal, which operates a family preservation program in California (see Appendix A), draws on the expertise of several consulting specialists to carry out various types of evaluations: physical, neurological, nutritional, and allergy examinations; blood chemistry evaluation; glucose tolerance test; speech and language evaluation; toxic metal screening; and psychological assessments, with a focus on ability to learn.

Disengagement. Disengagement—the process of terminating from the service—actually begins from day one. The practitioner advises the family members of the short-term, intensive nature of the service and gives them the time frame the service will span. The goals must therefore be achievable within the time constraints. The short time frame can be most helpful in keeping the family focused on the priorities. Skills can be taught rapidly and progress can be made quickly.

Because of the intense nature of this service, the practitioner may spend as much time with a family in one or two months as would represent a year of more of traditional hour-long weekly sessions. An especially close and trusting relationship usually develops between the practitioner and the family. Largely because of this relationship, considerable progress can be made in a short time by families that were sometimes viewed by other agencies as hopeless.

It might be considered not only cruel but damaging to the family to end the service in a short time period, forcing it to start all over again with some other provider for longer-term follow-up, but this is not so:

Shorter-term interventions put parents in control much quicker and avoid dependency.

The intensity of family preservation services cannot be sustained by the worker or family over longer time periods.

Most of the major accomplishments of this type of

service are achieved in the few beginning weeks of the intervention.

The practitioner tells the family from the beginning that the service will terminate at a specific time, and the time frame is continually kept in focus during the course of the service. To continue to be considered trustworthy, the practitioner must deliver on his or her word and formally end the service at the stipulated time. Informal contacts may, and frequently do, subsequently occur. Families often call to let the practitioner know how they are doing. Although family preservation services are aimed at helping families become self-sufficient, some families, having completed the service, may need some brief assistance or simply encouragement when they face their next crisis. Most projects allow families to come back again for a "booster shot" if they need brief help. The service is not repeated, but the family may need one or two meetings or telephone contacts with the practitioner to obtain guidance, clarification, or help in setting goals or developing a strategy to resolve a problem. Most often the family needs only some encouragement.

Initial Focus

Emphasis on the Positive. Many of the families seen by family preservation services have little trust in social service or other helping systems. They lack hope that their situation can change for the better. They are often dependent on social service systems and feel powerless to become independent. They lack confidence in themselves and are unable to take charge of their lives.

One of the most important tasks of the practitioner is to instill a sense of hope in the family that their problems can be solved and life can be more rewarding. For families who have been through various health, mental health, and social service systems over many years, this can be an extremely challenging task. The practitioner impresses on the family that family preservation services are different from what they experienced in the past. Staff members are willing to come to their home and work nights and weekends if necessary to accommodate the family's schedule, and be on call 24 hours a day. Most importantly, the practitioner conveys the belief that change is possible and that the family can exercise control over its circumstances.

Sometimes a family feels so beaten down and helpless that it is unable to perceive many of the ways in which it is faring well or even excelling. When its abilities and competencies are recognized and pointed out, the family begins to feel good about itself and gain confidence in its abilities. From this vantage point, the family no longer feels powerless, but rather hopeful that it can move forward and make improvements in its life as a family and its place in the community.

Bringing empowerment philosophy to practice. Empowerment is a process in which a family realizes and begins to use its own power to achieve control over its own destiny [Pinderhughes 1983; Hasenfeld 1987]. Family empowerment promotes parental autonomy by helping families solve their own problems and become less dependent on the intervention of social service agencies. The result of empowerment is that families assume control of their lives and achieve the goals they have set for themselves.

Empowerment implies certain assumptions:

> That people have a right to direct their own lives
>
> That people want to control their own lives and can learn to do so
>
> That doing things for people can interfere with their learning to take control of their own lives
>
> That giving people skills, information, and encouragement helps them gain more control over their lives and build self-esteem

When family preservation service begins, child protective services have often been involved and the family may be angry at more intrusion into their lives. The practitioner makes it clear to the family that the family preservation service is not an arm of child protective services, juvenile services, the court, or any other government agency. Rather it is there to help the family so that government agencies will no longer find it necessary to be involved.

The family preservation service starts where the clients are and elicits their perceptions of the problems, rather than simply defining problems from the perspective of the government agencies. For example, a school may call protective services and present the family's problem as the child's not coming to school. The family, however, defines its problem as unemployment. The oldest child stays home from school to care for a younger sibling when the single mother is out looking for a job.

The practitioner encourages families to identify problems they want resolved and to set their own priorities, balancing them with the need to respond to a government agency's concern about the children. The empowerment philosophy puts the family in charge of determining how to achieve this balance. The practitioner helps the family to clarify and view problems from different perspectives and to identify a range of solutions. The decision-making is the family's responsibility.

Although most social workers would agree that empowering families is an important goal, caseloads are often too high for workers to have time to spend with families in ways that promote empowerment. For example, if a client is having difficulty in obtaining some type of health or mental health service for a family member, his or her social worker could call the agency involved and speak to a supervisor or the director to help resolve the problem. It would consume significantly more time for the worker to teach the client how to advocate for himself or herself in this situation.

The following techniques are used to empower families:

Asking what changes clients want, respecting their wishes when they don't want changes, and being their partner in achieving the results they do want

Paying attention to the details of what is important to clients

Looking to clients for what is next and where to go for it

Working with clients' goals, tapping their dreams

Asking the simple questions, not making assumptions, or lecturing

Giving the power, not withholding information

Consulting with clients on all points, not making decisions about people's lives, even the details, behind their backs

Always being respectful, having good manners

Being on time or informing clients you will be late, apologizing sincerely for the discourtesy of being late when it does happen

Being sensitive to your "invasion" of their space

Listening actively to all that is being said, especially incidental comments and closing remarks

Being attentive to clients no matter what is going on*

Middle Phase

Empowerment Strategies

Setting goals and priorities. The practitioner respects the family's right to set its own goals and priorities. Having collected important information through the assessment process, the practitioner, in sharing this information, can help the family to sort out where change is needed most and where to begin.

Formulating goals that can be measured makes it easier for the family members to track their progress. Increasing parenting skills, for example, is not a measurable goal. Assuring that children attend school every day, however, is specific and measurable. Time is also a consideration in setting goals and priorities. Some goals should be short-term and relatively easy to accomplish, so the family can quickly experience some successes. Goals that will require some type of assistance from the practitioner should be achievable within the time frame of the service. Others of a longer-term nature may reasonably only be started, but with a plan developed as to the actions, resources, and time frames needed for their achievement [Fox 1987].

When an agency identifies a priority goal for a family that the family does not see as a priority, a potential conflict is created. For example, a protective services investigation may have found that a single mother leaves her young children unattended in the apartment for several hours at a time. The priority set by protective services for the mother is to provide appropriate supervision and not leave the children alone in the apartment. The mother's priority, however, is to move herself and her children to better housing in a safer environment, and she sometimes leaves the children to look for housing. The practitioner can help the family understand the concern of the government agency, the consequences of not responding to it, and ways to

*Excerpted from materials of the Family Preservation Project, Beacon Counseling, Boston, Massachusetts.

meet the family priorities while satisfying the agency's concern. In this case example, the practitioner may try to link the family with an agency that provides drop-in child care so the mother can continue apartment hunting.

Helping the family to organize for change. After the major goals have been identified and a plan for achieving them has been developed, the next step is to help the family organize itself to ensure that the plan is carried out. Each family member must understand any tasks he or she has agreed to do and the time frame for completion. This is the time when extended family members, friends, and other supportive persons made known through the assessment may be asked to provide some type of help directed at achieving a particular goal. Family preservation services try to help families enlist the support of their natural helping networks, which can be of continuing assistance after family preservation service terminates. Families are helped to identify and gain access to both informal and formal supports, to have a range of options for seeking assistance in the future, if needed.

Some agencies recommend regular family meetings as an important way to improve organizational skills and check on progress. Extended family members and other support persons participating in the plan should be involved in organizational meetings. During meetings the family reviews its goals, assigns tasks to individuals, and reviews progress. Problems in task completion are identified and solutions to problems are developed. For example, relatives who have agreed to provide child care while a mother seeks employment must now determine which days and how many hours they will watch the younger children. The family may find there are still uncovered hours that have to be planned for, as well as the need for a back-up child care plan in case of an emergency. Working as a team, the family then seeks ways to deal with these issues. Regular family meetings provide a structure for the family members to begin to experience control over their lives and to take pride as a family in their accomplishments.

Organizing service providers. Besides helping the family to organize itself, it may be necessary to organize service providers that are involved with the family. Sometimes several organizations, such as the school guidance department, public health, mental health, social service, corrections, and substance abuse treatment, may be working with various family members at cross-purposes with one another. It is confusing to families when service providers are saying different things and there is no collaboration. Families can get stuck and end up doing nothing if they are not sure whose direction they should be following. Bringing all the services together with the family can be useful in advising the providers of the overall plan and major goals, and determining how the providers can participate in the plan. It may become obvious that all the services are not needed.

In the absence of collaboration or in the face of past failures, there may be a tendency to put more and more services into a family, when actually fewer are needed. Collaboration can best be determined when it is decided which services are most closely related to the priority goals in the plan, how services can be scheduled for the family's convenience, how information will be transmitted, how services will be monitored and evaluated, and which agency will take the role of case manager. Child protective services, if involved with the family, would likely assume the case management function because of its authority and responsibility to ensure protection of the child. As goals are achieved or the family's situation changes, service needs may change. Decisions governing the use of services are made by the family with help from the family preservation practitioner.

Linkages/advocacy. One of the roles of the practitioner is to link the family with supportive services to achieve the goals they have set. For example, a mother may require day care for a young child so she can find employment. Other supportive services include home health aides, homemakers, parent aides, parent education, vocational training, and substance abuse treatment. Families often do not have information on the range of community-based services available to them. Linking families with community services reduces their isolation and opens new options and possibilities for improving the quality of their lives.

Information alone is not always sufficient to enable a family to reach out beyond its own borders. Families may be fearful or uncertain about how to approach a community resource. Past experience may lead them to anticipate rejection or a negative response, and they prefer to avoid such a situation. If family members are to learn how to cope with problems or crises in the future, they must learn how to find and gain access to needed supports. Once they have mastered these skills, they are no longer helpless in the face of a crisis.

Although time-consuming, teaching families to advocate for themselves is one of the most important functions of the practitioner. Hours may be spent role-playing and rehearsing with parents how they will deal with housing, public assistance, Medicaid, and the schools. Time is also spent accompanying clients to interviews and sitting in waiting rooms to give encouragement and moral support while the client learns and practices negotiating service systems.

We know from our experience and research that professional interventions alone do not always help families. They often require the additional buttressing of support from informal helping networks. In some communities informal supports are the main form of help because few professional services exist or are accessible. Family preservation practitioners must be able to help families identify and mobilize these informal networks.

Whittaker et al. [1989] have identified critical questions a practitioner will need to pose, and have developed assessment tools for this purpose. The following are the main questions:

What kinds of support does the family need?

Who in the family's network is willing to do what to assist the family?

What are the impediments to this help?

How can they be removed?

How can more help be mobilized if needed?

How can it be kept going?

Counseling/therapy. Family preservation services are family-centered. No particular member is singled out as "the problem"; the problems or difficulties experienced by any one member affect the whole family, and vice versa. The practitioner may at times work with the entire family, including extended family members and family friends, or with subgroups of the family or with individual members. No "right way" or particular therapeutic model has been shown to work best in family preservation services; practitioners may draw upon structural, cognitive, behavioral, or other approaches.

Once concrete needs have been met, the family is able to look into whatever else is keeping them from achieving the goals they want. The practitioner helps the family members to reframe or view problems in different ways so they can formulate new solutions. Providing supportive counseling to help an individual family member through the performance of a task or to achieve a certain goal may be a focus of the practitioner's intervention. If an individual requires long-term therapy, a referral is made to another provider.

Concrete services. It is an important feature of family preservation programs that they respond quickly to help a family meet concrete and basic needs such as food, clothing, shelter, gas and electric supply, transportation, and babysitting. Programs usually set aside funds for quick handling of emergencies and for purchasing essential goods and services for the family. Linkages are also made with community organizations that provide concrete assistance to families, such as furniture, clothing, or food. Providing tangible goods and services is a way of demonstrating good faith to the family and sending a message that the project wants to be helpful.

Education/skill-building. Part of the empowerment process involves the family's acquiring the knowledge and skills it needs for daily living, coping with crises, and achieving its goals. Family preservation services help families learn skills such as communication, discipline without violence, household management, and assertiveness. Workers teach and model new skills and behaviors. If more formalized training or education is needed, such as job training or GED, the family preservation service worker is responsible for helping the family member to locate and gain access to the appropriate source.

Considerations in the Middle Phase

Continued assessment and case planning. The middle phase is a very active and energetic period because practitioner and family members are working to accomplish goals within the brief time period of the service. As the family increasingly trusts the practitioner, more of the family secrets are revealed. A drinking problem or previous sexual abuse that was not evident at intake may become known. The practitioner continually reassesses whether the children are safe in the home. New information as well as new events or crises may change the assessment. As family tasks are accomplished or not accomplished, the practitioner examines with the family whether goals need to be revised or different strategies need to be developed.

Realistic expectations. During the reassessments of the original plan, it will become clear whether the original expectations were realistic. It may be that the original plan was too extensive for the amount of time available in the family preservation service. Some tasks may not be progressing as rapidly as had been anticipated. Rather than perceiving this as failure, the practitioner and the family need to appreciate and take pride in the positive changes that have been made. Within that positive framework, the family then works on revising its goals and expectations of what can be accomplished by the end of the family preservation service.

Sometimes the practitioner, more than the family, feels disappointed that original expectations have not been realized. He or she may have been overly optimistic in the beginning about how rapidly the family would progress. It is important that the worker appreciate the changes that have taken place and encourage and participate in the family's pride in its accomplishments.

Ending Phase

Achieving Stability

During this last phase the family completes the transition from dependence on family preservation services to independence. The family members now have a broader set of skills that will help them to cope with problems or crises in the future. They know more about what community and informal resources are available and how to reach them. They are more able to express feelings and deal with conflicts among themselves. Parents are more in charge and are better able to nurture the children, as well as set limits. Since part of the family's work in family preservation services was to build a network of support, family members are no longer as isolated. If problems arise, they now can call on a broad range of resources from extended family members to community-based organizations to get whatever kind of support they need.

Although these improvements have been made, the family's circumstances are not ideal. Not all of its problems have been settled. Sometimes, just before termination, problems seem to escalate. This can be expected. As the end of the service draws near, the family may panic and show some regression. The practitioner works through fears with family members, helping them to see that they have many more skills and options for handling problems than they did before. Several sessions with the family should be devoted to talking about the imminent termination; this part of family preservation service intervention needs time for acceptance to develop.

Some families will continue to need ongoing support for a period of time after family preservation service is terminated. Although the family has weathered the crisis and has remained intact, it may have only begun to work on some problems, such as substance abuse, that require continued help. The practitioner is responsible for seeing that the family is linked with appropriate follow-up services before termination.

Letting Go

The worker begins to prepare the family for disengaging from the service from the very first family interview. Throughout the course of the service the worker keeps the family focused on the brief time frame in which they will work together. Even with this preparation, termination is difficult for the family, as well as for the practitioner.

Families continually face endings, as well as new beginnings. Moving from a cherished home to a new neighborhood, changing jobs, seeing the children leave home—all involve letting go. The worker helps the family members see that they are strong enough to let go of the service, and that ending is a life experience they will continue to encounter.

References

Fox, Raymond. "Short-Term Goal-Oriented Family Therapy." *Social Casework* 68, 8 (October 1987).

Hartman, Ann, and Laird, Joan. *Family Centered Social Work Practice.* New York: The Free Press, 1983.

Hasenfeld, Yeheskel. "Power in Social Work Practice." *Social Service Review* 61, 3 (September 1987): 469–483.

Intensive Family Services: A Family Preservation Service Delivery Model. Baltimore, MD: Maryland Department of Human Resources, 1987.

Lippit, Gordon, and Lippit, Donald. *The Consulting Process.* La Jolle, CA: University Associates, Inc., 1978.

Pinderhughes, Elaine B. "Empowerment for Our Clients and for Ourselves." *Social Casework* 64, 6 (June 1983): 331–338.

Whittaker, James; Tracy, Elizabeth; and Marckworth, Margaret. *Family Support Project.* Seattle, WA: The University of Washington School of Social Work, 1989.

4

Administrative Considerations

Creating relevant and effective family preservation services and installing them within an organization and a community require a number of informed administrative decisions. Some choices are difficult. Most are complex. All are interrelated. Consequences are both obvious and subtle. This section points up principle decision points and options and their possible consequences and implications. The issues form four categories: Program Design; Staffing; Selecting a Service Delivery System; and Other Administrative Considerations.

Program Design

There are 13 major program design elements to be planned and established: Eligibility Criteria; Target Populations; Service Mix; Flexible Funds to Meet Concrete Needs; Service Site; Flexibility—Working Hours, Staff Roles; Duration of Service; Caseload Size and Intensity of Service; Staffing Patterns; Treatment Models; Linkages; Advocacy Component; and Paperwork and Forms.

Eligibility Criteria

Selecting which cases are eligible and how and when eligibility will be determined are critical decision points. The following are key considerations:

Is the service needed? Is there imminent risk of removal of a child from the family? Is the child already outside the home?

Can a less intensive intervention suffice?

Has less intensive help been offered but was not effective?

Is the family a safe place for all its members and the helper?

Can the family benefit from this help? Are the members willing and able to engage in the process?

Were these determinations made recently by an individual who had face-to-face contact with the family?

As described in Chapter 1, family preservation services target families whose children are at imminent risk of being removed from their homes and placed in substitute care. Clearly defining imminent risk so that workers can easily identify and select the most appropriate cases to refer to this service is not a simple task. Cases in which children are at imminent risk of placement may look different from community to community, based on available resources, intensity of social problems, minimum community standards for adequate child care, and so forth. Some programs have established review teams to determine whether referred cases are at imminent risk of placement and meet other criteria.

Factors to consider in determining imminent risk include:

1.   *Likelihood and severity of threatened harm.*

The greater the likelihood and severity of threatened harm, the greater the risk of placement.

2.   *Immediacy of threatened harm.*

The more immediate the threatened harm, the greater the risk of placement. For example, harm would be more immediate to infants whose mothers are not feeding them regularly than to 12-year-olds.

3.   *Decision of authorized agent to place a child.*

A child should be considered by a family preservation service to be at imminent risk of placement if a person authorized to make placements, such as a judge, or a representative from the department of social services or the department of mental health, decides that the child should be placed in substitute care. A family preservation service may disagree with the referring agency that a particular case is serious enough to warrant intensive, in-home crisis intervention service. Without the intervention of family preservation services, however, the placement agency will remove the child from the home. The child is at imminent risk of placement by virtue of the agency's decision to place the child.

4.   *Perceived time frame in which placement will occur.*

The more immediate the time frame in which placement will likely occur, the more imminent the risk of placement. Some agencies, for example, set a particular time period— such as 48 hours, one week, two weeks—to define "imminent." If a placement is judged likely to occur within the set time period, the risk of placement is considered imminent.

The evaluation process should include measures that assess potential harm to the child at home, the psychological harm of removal, and the salutary effects of family preservation service in reducing the potential harm.

Target Populations: Who Can Benefit from Help?

Those newly charged with the responsibility to develop family preservation services often ask questions such as, "What groups can benefit from a family preservation service? Does it work for delinquents or families abusing drugs or alcohol?" There are no pat answers to these difficult questions. Family preservation services have been used with a wide variety of client populations in which children were at risk of placement. The following are examples of factors associated with risk of placement:

> Abuse and/or neglect of children
> Emotional disturbance of children
> Severe parent-child conflict
> Aggressive/assaultive/acting out behavior of children
> Homelessness
> Substance abuse
> Environmental problems

Rather than ask what types of cases or problems are best helped by family preservation services, one should ask: Can this case benefit from a short-term, crisis intervention service? In this framework no group or specific client population is automatically eliminated; rather, cases are screened in relation to whether they need crisis intervention service or some other type of service.

An agency may, however, want to direct its family preservation services to particular types of cases that appear to be at higher risk of placement than others. Examining a sample of cases that have recently entered care will yield information for the agency to determine trends and characteristics of the families and children receiving placement services. Factors such as age of child, family composition, previous involvement with the agency, reasons for placement, and abuse of drugs or alcohol, can be useful in profiling populations at greatest risk. For example, if the analysis reveals that a large percentage of foster care placements are infants and preschoolers of young parents, or adolescents with emotional problems, family preservation services might then be directed, although not necessarily limited, to those groups.

In defining a target population, another issue to consider is whether the service will focus on new cases coming into the system, cases that have been in the system for a long time but have not been successfully helped, or a mixture of both. Some family preservation service projects have chosen to use their limited staffs only with cases new to the system. Limited staff resources are allocated to cases that are presumed to have a greater likelihood of success.

The fact that a case is new does not mean that the family's problems are new. Often the problems are long-standing, but some change in the family's situation and ability to manage the problems has led to a crisis. Because the case is new, the family does not have a history of past failures or a history of negative experiences with the agency that have engendered cynicism or hostility toward the agency that first must be overcome.

Some family preservation projects, however, have elected to take cases after every other agency service has failed. In this approach, the family preservation service becomes the service of last resort. The expectation is that families will quickly realize that this service is quite different from the services they previously received. Resistance or hostility can soon be overcome. The highest intensity of service is therefore retained for the most difficult cases.

At times, cases of lesser difficulty may be assigned for training family preservation staff members. For example, the New Jersey Division of Youth and Family Services began to purchase family preservation services from four private agency providers in four different counties. None of the staff members in any of these agencies had ever delivered family preservation services before. For teaching purposes and to avoid overwhelming new staff members with the most complex cases, New Jersey established a "continuum of family preservation service eligibility criteria." Family preservation programs began opening cases using the first two of the following criteria; as staff members became more experienced, programs gradually incorporated the additional eligibility criteria.

> Children who are at imminent risk of first-time out-of-home placement
>
> Children who currently are in temporary placement less than 30 days
>
> Children who currently are, or who in the past were, in placement less than 90 days
>
> Children living at home and at imminent risk of placement who were previously in placement for no more than six months
>
> Children living at home and at imminent risk of placement who have previously been in shelter, detention, or foster care placement of any kind for any duration

Programs may establish different eligibility criteria according to various factors, such as size of the program, requirements of funding sources, experience and expertise of the staff, and program philosophy. For example, a program with only a few staff members may want to narrow the scope of the population it serves, whereas a larger program may accept a broader population. Some programs may be funded by a particular agency to take referrals only from that agency.

The procedure for determining eligibility should emphasize that these decisions not be based solely on referral reports or past evaluations. Although these may be reviewed and given some consideration, the more important information comes from current face-to-face contacts with the family.

Clear written criteria and procedures should be established for case acceptance and rejection; how organizational units will communicate decisions; what levels of the staff will be involved; and how disputes will be settled.

Service Mix

Family preservation services incorporate a mix of counseling, advocacy, educational, skill-building, and concrete service activities, (food, clothing, shelter, transportation). Administrators need to (1) establish a way to describe for the community what those existing services are; and (2) design an administrative process to make them readily accessible to the family. Care should be taken to simplify procedures.

Flexible Funds to Meet Concrete Needs

Most family preservation service programs have built into their budget some discretionary funding that can be used to meet a family's emergency needs. Policies governing the use of these funds should clarify their purpose, restrictions on their use, and the circumstances under which workers can use them directly or will require approval from a higher authority. It is critically important that policy enable funds to be used immediately to respond to an emergency. Larger public and private agencies may need to develop a streamlined fiscal procedure for this purpose.

It is also important that family preservation services incorporate counseling and educational help *and* also concrete services. Unless this service mix is clearly part of the program design, some service providers will see themselves as delivering only the "talk therapy" component and not the hard services, because they have never done the latter in the past.

Service Site

Another new experience for family preservation service providers may be the delivery of services in the family home or natural environment. Although organizations may have delivered "services to children in their own homes" or "community-based alternatives," most often these services were delivered in the organization's offices. Working with the families in their own homes offers multiple benefits for both the family and the practitioner. Meeting in the family home, a setting that is comfortable and convenient for the family, promotes family empowerment. In the home, the family is in charge and the practitioner is a guest, whereas an office setting underscores the authority of the practitioner. Coming to the home and making the service convenient to the family is one way of illustrating that the service is designed to be as helpful as possible. The practitioner who spends considerable time with the family in its own environment gets a comprehensive view and understanding of the family, both in terms of its own interactions and its interactions with the larger community.

To break long-ingrained patterns, an administrative policy should clearly state that office visits are the exception rather than the rule and spell out the circumstances when they might possibly be allowed.

Flexibility—Working Hours, Staff Roles

Family preservation staff members have irregular working hours. Because they meet with families at the families' convenience, they may work in the evenings or on weekends. Because of the crisis nature of the service, they must be available to the family when the family needs their help. Policies concerning working hours must grant flexibility both in terms of allowing for evening and weekend work and emergencies, and allowing for fluctuations in the total number of hours worked in a given week. An agency may, for example, require employees to work a 40-hour week. If a response to a family crisis results in a workweek of 50 hours, the following workweek should be reduced to 30 hours. Granting this type of flexibility is not generally a problem for private agencies, but may require some exceptions or waivers in a public agency that is bound by civil service rules and/or a union contract. Administrative policy also should specify what additional demands will be made on the staff to ensure 24-hour daily coverage, and how staff members will be compensated for their time.

Staff roles must be flexible to enable the staff to respond to a family's immediate needs, allowing the staff to model new behaviors for families and teach new skills. A social worker, for example, may want to go grocery shopping with a mother and her young child to teach such skills as money management, nutrition, and nonviolent discipline, as well as using the driving time for supportive counseling. Grocery shopping would likely be in the job description for an aide rather than a social worker, but in a nontraditional service that is provided in the family's home, rigid distinctions between various staff roles and responsibilities must be allowed to blur. While families are being taught a range of options with which to respond to life stresses, the staff members must also be allowed to exercise a wide variety of options in responding to the needs of the families they serve.

Duration of Service

Choices about service duration and service objectives affect costs. Making informed decisions about the duration of a service requires conscious choices about the purpose of the service. For example: Are the goals limited to the core objectives of safety, avoidance of unnecessary placement, and enough family stability to ensure both these objectives, or are they to extend to improved parenting and family life?

The briefest intervention involves only the core objectives. If necessary, the extended family and the community—formal and informal helpers—are viewed as sources of continuing help, and linkage is made to them during treatment. Moderate-length intervention (to six months) and long-term (six months or more) tend to go beyond core objectives to more improved family functioning; they combine crisis service and aftercare service or provide crisis service and monitoring of progress.

For the most part, brief intervention services rely on the family to request further help from the agency after the services are completed; subsequent contact is minimal. Moderate to long-term services monitor the family over a longer period of time and determine ongoing needs to be addressed. The longer the staff is involved with the family, the greater the potential for the family to become dependent.

The nature and amount of program funding may sometimes exert greater influence than the needs of clients on discussions concerning service duration. At this point, no research has been published comparing the relative effectiveness of brief, moderate, and long-term service approaches. Evaluations indicate, however, that brief intervention is effective in achieving core objectives.

Caseload Size and Intensity of Service

Caseload size and intensity of service are integrally related. The effectiveness of family preservation services derives in large part from its intensity, accessibility, and flexibility in relation to client need and therapeutic opportunity. The ideal caseload is two families at a time for a single practitioner. Larger caseloads limit the practitioner's ability to give the intensity of attention required by a family in crisis for defusing potentially violent situations; developing and implementing safety plans; responding to emergencies, such as an eviction; teaching skills such as communication, stress management, and assertiveness; and gaining access to community resources. Low caseloads are a prerequisite to achieving the core objectives of safety and avoidance of unnecessary placement.

Staffing Patterns

Three basic staffing patterns are common in family preservation programs: single practitioner, copractitioner, and practitioner-paraprofessional team. The choice of staffing pattern is influenced by the following considerations:

Which pattern most closely expresses the agency's program philosophy?

Which may better serve the agency's clients?

Which is most congruent with the agency's treatment model?

Which can best be staffed and supported within the agency's administrative structure?

Which is most cost effective?

Single practitioner. This pattern consists of a primary practitioner involved with the family from the beginning to the end of the service, supported by a peer and supervisory consultation team as well as a back-up practitioner who may participate in the case at any time he or she is needed. The back-up practitioner is introduced to the family early in the process.

Those who have chosen this pattern believe that it has certain advantages for clients and staff members over the other patterns:

It is less intrusive than the other patterns—a particular advantage in a time of crisis and confusion.

One practitioner can gain the family's trust easier than several.

It eliminates the problem of different practitioners taking sides with various family members.

The practitioner can be spontaneous in taking advantage of natural therapeutic opportunities because there is no need to consult with or consider another practitioner.

Most energy can go into client issues, not colleague issues.

Administrative considerations include:

Less cost

More focused accountability

Simpler management

Higher efficiency

Emphasis on selection of skilled and experienced practitioners

Need for regular peer and supervisory consultation to share perspectives, plan strategies, give support and feedback

Immediate back-up practitioner and supervisor access

Plan for exceptional circumstances such as illness or other unavailability of the primary practitioner

Copractitioner. In this model, two practitioners share responsibility for assessment, provision of short-term therapy, and if needed, case management.

Those who have chosen this pattern believe that it offers distinct advantages:

A second practitioner provides another perspective in assessing family problems and strengths and helping sort out the often-complex dynamics.

The copractitioner raises questions, challenges assumptions, offers different viewpoints, confirms observations, and offers feedback on new techniques or intervention strategies.

Copractitioners can also provide emotional support to each other in times of discouragement, and can share satisfactions, thereby reducing the potential for staff burnout.

This model offers a natural back-up system in case one

therapist is not able to continue with the family. Transitions are easier, and a new person does not have to be introduced.

Administrative considerations include:

Higher costs than the single practitioner pattern
Shared accountability
Reliable, efficient back-up system in place
More complex management:
Matching copractitioners for approach and styles
Resolving case-control issues and other disagreements
More time and effort required to work together, determine strategies, clarify roles, give feedback and support, jointly assess and reassess
Supervision still required to consult, support, and assess team issues as well as case issues

Practitioner-paraprofessional. Some projects have chosen to team a practitioner with a parent-aide or other paraprofessional. The paraprofessional provides a range of supportive services.

The paraprofessional often has a primary role in providing parenting education and linkages with other community resources; especially in families in which abuse or neglect has occurred, the paraprofessional may teach child care skills, appropriate methods of discipline, and communication skills. The paraprofessional helps to reduce the isolation of the family by identifying community resources and linking families to them. The paraprofessional can also become involved in working with the family on concrete needs, such as housing. Considerable time must often be spent in dealing with housing personnel, landlords, shelters, utility companies, etc. Families need guidance in how to reach and negotiate with them. The services of the paraprofessional free the practitioner to concentrate on family interactions, communication, and other patterns that are preventing the family from achieving its goals.

The paraprofessional often spends considerable time with the family and is likened to a close friend. The paraprofessional sometimes is from the same community, or shares the same culture or ethnicity as the family. The family may identify more closely with the paraprofessional than with the practitioner, and develop a close and personal relationship. With the building of trust, the family becomes more comfortable in sharing information with the paraprofessional and revealing feelings and concerns.

Many of the same advantages ascribed to the copractitioner pattern are present also in the practitioner-paraprofessional model. Administrative considerations include:

Higher cost than the single practitioner pattern

Importance of defining job roles in ways that allow for flexibility and some overlap

Allowance for sufficient time for teamwork to determine strategies, clarify roles, give feedback and support, coordinate schedules, and jointly assess and reassess

Supervisory and consultant time required on team issues in addition to case issues

Treatment Models

Research and experience show that organizations plan for most aspects of a program design and then omit or leave to chance a pivotal factor—what treatment or change technology will be used? What theoretical models will be applied? Cognitive, behavioral, structural models? Family systems? Social learning? A combination with ecological emphasis?

Although most family preservation services operate within a particular theoretical framework, practitioners often borrow techniques and approaches from other theories that may be useful for a given family.

The task of the administrator is to see that treatment approaches:

Are suitable for short-term, intensive, in-home intervention

Are consistent with the values of family preservation, that is, empowerment, respect for the family

Work with specific client groups in need of service (particularly if clients are poor, or of diverse cultures)

Provide for concrete services

Are congruent with the knowledge and skills of the staff members who are to deliver the service

Promote a nonhierarchical relationship between practitioner and client

Are appropriate to the caseload size

Linkages

Family preservation services are crisis-triggered. Other assistance should be available to families who may need it before a crisis occurs and after it is over. Administrators have to plan and implement how early intervention, crisis intervention, and follow-up services will be linked. Administrative tasks include:

Surveying existing programs and client needs; determining if needs and services are congruent and where gaps exist

Establishing ongoing methods of identifying resources and establishing formal procedures for gaining access to them, and incorporating them into written agreements

Creating and implementing a plan to obtain needed resources that do not yet exist

Issues administrators can anticipate and compensate for include:

A tendency to use the crisis service as a substitute for earlier or less intensive services

An inclination to keep crisis cases open and provide follow-up services rather than to refer and/or terminate— tendencies that can be controlled by eligibility policies specifying crisis cases, time frames for case closings, and a process for monitoring and reviewing cases that will check for conformance to policy

Advocacy Component

The social workers' code of ethics impels them to work on negative environmental factors that affect their clients. Other professions engaged in family preservation work may not have the same obligation in their code of ethics, but should be compelled by the logic that intrafamilial improvement will be impossible to achieve and sustain in a toxic social environment. Who best should advocate but those professions that have an intimate acquaintance with the effects that poor housing, health, employment, education—in short, poverty—have on families. Administrators can foster advocacy and social change in the following ways:

Incorporating social change as a part of the organization's mission statement

Including advocacy as a part of all staff job descriptions

Including an advocacy agenda in the plan for the organization. This could include a range of activities: collecting information on social conditions that affect clients negatively; publishing papers on the topic; informing the public through the media and conferences; petitioning and lobbying local, state or provincial, and federal governments. The organization may carry out the activities or link with other state or national advocacy organizations with a primary focus on this agenda.

Paperwork and Forms

The usual strictures about paper work and forms apply to those used by family preservation programs. They should be pertinent; kept to a minimum; simple and clear; capable of being understood by the people who fill them out; and not duplicative.

Reports and forms used by family preservation services should not only capture information on the individual members but on the family as such. Forms should complement and support a family-focused approach to assessment and treatment. Family preservation service practitioners assess the family as a whole but must often use agency forms or Medicaid forms that require per-individual information; they were not designed to capture family-centered data. Administrators should adapt existing forms to a family focus. This may be difficult, time-consuming, or even impossible to achieve for some state or federal forms. The staff should be given guidelines on how to incorporate family data into existing forms.

Staffing

Finding Qualified Staff Members

One activity that often delays program start-up is the recruitment and hiring of qualified staff members. The time required for this activity should not be underestimated. A minimum of three months will likely be needed. It is often difficult to find staff members who have appropriate academic qualifications, share the values of family preservation, have experience working with families, bring excitement and enthusiasm to this type of work, and are willing and able to work flexible hours. Projects—particularly those in rural areas— report difficulty in finding experienced candidates. Projects in urban areas report that some candidates are fearful about going into homes in neighborhoods they consider unsafe. Agencies find that some candidates do not want to commit themselves to evening and weekend work and 24-hour on-call duty. There is not a ready pool of applicants to draw from. Schools of social work, psychology, and counseling are not generally preparing students for this type of work.

Although suitable recruitment is difficult, it is by no means impossible. Methods often include advertising in local newspapers and professional and association newsletters; increasing awareness about this type of employment opportunity through state or school-sponsored job fairs; asking current family practitioners whether associates or friends are interested; and talking about the program to classes of graduate schools in social work, psychology, and education.

It is wise for agencies to begin discussions with graduate school administrators as far in advance as possible of actually developing a family preservation program. The schools may be able to supply student interns for the program who then become likely candidates for employment. Once the schools understand the nature of the service and are convinced of the potential employment market for their students, they are likely to become quite interested in developing a role as a training resource.

Some family preservation projects have set the salaries and vacation time for staff members higher than the average for comparable master's-level positions. The higher salary and vacation time help compensate for evening and weekend work, in addition, of course, to averaging the workweek, thus making the positions more competitive. Some of the positive aspects emphasized in recruitment include flexible working hours, ability to work independently, low caseloads, staff supports such as training and consultation, and most importantly, the resources and ability to help people make significant changes in a short time.

Staff Screening and Selection

The success of the program, for the most part, depends on the quality and capabilities of the staff. Generally, family preservation services try to recruit master's-level staff members for practitioner positions. It is important for the staff to have had the academic and clinical training to assess risk to the children; family dynamics, problems, and strengths; and to design interventions that will help the families achieve their goals. Although training is usually provided for new staff members in family preservation programs, it is a supplement to, rather than a substitute for, previous training and experience.

Because staff selection is so critical, the process for selecting staff members should allow sufficient time to get to know candidates, view their capabilities, and understand their attitudes about families. This generally involves not only face-to-face interviews, but involvement of candidates in role-playing, simulation of a family session, evaluation of hypothetical case situations; and value-clarification exercises. Screening of applicants should be rigorous.

Prospective employees should be given a detailed job description that outlines duties and responsibilities. Current staff members can embellish written materials by descriptions of their practice. At that point some applicants will screen themselves out.

When asked, a number of family preservation service program administrators and supervisors listed the following attributes that make a "good practitioner":

Clinically skilled and knowledgeable in the agency's practice model, or skilled and willing to learn
Profamily—a commitment to family stability
Likes both adults and children
Believes in the capacity of people to grow and change
Good listener

Nonjudgmental

Does not take sides

Creative and resourceful

Flexible

Sense of humor

Sense of adventure—not frightened by different people and situations

Low need to control others

Ability to deal with ambiguity

Able to reduce the emotional distance between self and the client

Will also "do windows, help clean, or paint" if client needs this kind of assistance

Self-directed

Ability to adapt quickly to unfamiliar situations and circumstances

Genuine desire to help others

Supervisory Staff

Nature of supervision. Supervision in family preservation programs serves the same basic, critical functions as in other services:

To enable the employee to perform the tasks or deliver the service of the organization

To ensure that tasks and services are managed and performed according to the organization's mission, policies, and values, within time limits

To evaluate the practitioner's performance

Yet those who do supervise family preservation work feel that it is different. How does it differ? Family preservation supervision must use the same qualities between supervisor and practitioner as exist between the practitioner and the family. Supervision is intense, accessible, focused. A supervisor's role includes supporting, empowering, and training, as well as managing.

Intensity. Supervisors report spending more time with practitioners than is typical. The brevity of the service, the severe crises, the need to plan and strategize, all require more frequent and longer supervisory sessions.

Accessibility. The 24-hour accessibility of the practitioner to the client requires that supervisors be available to the practitioner on the same basis. In the single-practitioner pattern, the supervisor is often used as the support team member or back-up practitioner to the family.

Focus. Because of the chaos in the families they see, practitioners easily and quickly become inundated with information and conflicting messages that are difficult to sort out. Helping staff members sift out the useful information is a major supervisory task.

The families have no shortage of problems that need attention. Identifying a set of core objectives is a difficult mission for staff members and families. The supervisor, as an objective reviewer, can more easily determine whether the objectives are those the family both wants and needs to achieve, and whether they can be accomplished by a family preservation service.

Supervisors begin by assuring that the intervention is focused on limited objectives, and continue as the case moves on to make sure that the activities are targeted to the objectives. Because this is a brief intervention, each visit must be purposefully related to the objectives. In short, supervisors must spend extra time helping staff members to find the focus and stay on it.

Empowering. Supervisors must believe that practitioners have both the desire and the capacity to do the work. If practitioners lack either or both, supervisors cannot empower them to do the job. Most practitioners and families can succeed and any approach to either that assumes failure is bound to result in it.

Although critical lessons are conveyed in the intellectual discussion of cases, they are most effectively conveyed through the supervisor's perspective and attitudes toward the family and practitioner. By using techniques that promote empowerment for workers, supervisors model for them how they should act with families. This approach requires that the supervisors treat workers with respect, and do not put them into situations where they will lose face with peers, superiors, or clients. It requires that they help staff members set objectives for their work; coach practitioners to do tasks but do not do the work for them; and have staff members identify the areas of their work that need improvement.

Supportive and nurturing work with crisis-ridden families drains staff members of energy and is sometimes overwhelming. Supervisors have to offer a great deal of support. Workers tend to overlook gains that are made and to minimize their own role in them. Supervisors should be quick to spot accomplishments and be generous with praise.

Some supervisors have weekly unit meetings where practitioners can be debriefed, let off steam, and receive support from peers. Having a regular unit lunch away from the office is a reward and a respite. Staff parties, birthday celebrations, special events, and holidays all reinforce the sense that staff members are cared about and appreciated. Supervisors should monitor the physical and emotional fatigue of their workers and make sure that they take time off. This appears to be a problem for some staff members; supervisors often have to insist that a staff member take vacation or sick time.

As noted earlier, it is necessary to closely monitor brief crisis-intervention services. Unless this is done, case activities can drift. Tracking progress is a primary task for the supervisor. Cases are often hard to end because much could still be done, and because practitioners often are the source of the first positive help many families have received. There may well be a strong tendency to carry on with the case when the planned goals have been reached. Supervisors help staff members to terminate service appropriately.

Teaching. Supervisors also help workers with their skills and knowledge. Since these are best acquired by doing, supervisors in many agencies often carry a case or two to preserve and sharpen skills. It keeps supervisors tuned in to the realities of the pressures and complexities in the caseloads. It also provides another avenue for the supervisor to teach through modeling.

Managing. An agency is more than a loose band of private practitioners. It is created by or under laws that require that its purpose be explicit. Most agencies have written and unwritten policies that illustrate how they are to achieve their missions. It is an essential function of supervision to ensure that the work of the staff is done in accord with the agency's mission and policies.

Supervisors are in a position to see how effective or relevant the agency's policies are. Their job description should include responsibility for reporting to administrators on which policies should be eliminated or changed and which should be initiated. They are also the prime interpreters of agency policy. It is here that the supervisors' values and those of the agency take on added importance. Values are the lens one looks through in translating policy. The selection and training of supervisors, as well as practitioners, should stress the identification and discussion of the values that have been discussed in preceding chapters.

Supervisors are responsible for putting together an overall evaluation of a worker's performance. How well are families served? How well did the employee function as a member of this organization?

Personnel reports in many kinds of organizations are unilateral; the supervisor or the evaluator writes the report, employees merely agree or disagree. The ethos of social work, including family preservation services, dictates another approach. Not only must the practitioners participate fully in the evaluation of their work, but clients should also evaluate the service they received. The purpose of the evaluation in this light is not only to reward strength but to identify areas where practitioners can improve performance.

In several family preservation service agencies, practitioners also evaluate supervisors and administrators. Just as clients are the best judges of whether they have been helped by a service, staff members are the best judges of whether supervision and administration have helped them.

Problems of supervision.   Family preservation service supervisors are vulnerable to the perennial problems of supervision: overprotecting or underprotecting practitioners, becoming agency-driven rather than service-driven, and being overwhelmed.

We have already mentioned that one of the ways supervisors fail to empower practitioners is to do for them what they should be doing for themselves. Sometimes supervisors do this because they want to protect practitioners from difficult situations or those that they feel the practitioners will not handle well, or sometimes they are afraid, rightly or wrongly, that too much risk is involved for the client if they leave it to the worker. The message this gives to a practitioner is the same negative one a practitioner can give to a family or a parent or a child when this approach is used: "I really don't think you are capable of doing this the way it should be done." As a result, practitioners become dependent or hostile, or most likely both.

The desire to take over and do the work may stem from supervisors' wishes to provide the service themselves. Most supervisors are drawn from provider ranks and some may want to do what they liked and felt they could do best. Whatever the cause, the price paid because of overprotective supervisors is too high. This is perhaps another reason why it makes good sense for supervisors to carry a case of their own.

At the other end of the continuum is the underprotective supervisor—the one who fails to recognize the risks and pressures in this work and does not support the practitioners. It is a common supervisory failing to distance oneself emotionally from the practitioner. When practitioners lack acknowledgment of, and assistance to work through, their feelings, they may model the supervisor's behavior and distance themselves from their clients.

Another frequent shortcoming of supervision is the failure to provide the teaching, consultation, or skill-building a staff member may need. Lacking the ability or desire to do this, the supervisors become service controllers of sorts. Their main interests are in quotas, how many cases, how much time, what outcomes. Although these interests are vital to their role as managers, they should not supersede the role of teacher-trainer.

Finally, the most serious problem in regard to supervision occurs when supervisors are not adequately chosen, prepared, or supported. Not all superior service-delivery staff members automatically make good supervisors. Those chosen should be capable of, and willing to, manage and evaluate the work of others. This requires that the agency establish some advancement track whereby senior workers can be provided with the same pay levels and status as managers, so that promotion into management is not the only way a staff member can make more money and achieve higher status.

Once chosen to supervise or manage, supervisors should be provided with training to reinforce values, upgrade skills and knowledge, and encompass administrative aspects of the supervisors' evaluation function. Administration should provide for supervisors the equivalent of what supervisors are expected to provide their workers.

Training/Consultation/Support

To ensure effective services and promote retention of staff, the agency must make a commitment to staff training and other kinds of staff support. The training should be designed according to staff members' needs, taking into account their level of knowledge and skill in working with families. Philosophy and values should be incorporated into the skills-development training.

In some instances, staff members may be experienced family therapists, but may not have worked in the home or with this target population; or the staff members may be experienced clinicians, but may not have worked with the family as a unit. The training should be flexible enough to address various levels of skill. The following are examples of topics that might be included in initial training:

Family Systems Theory
Family Therapy Techniques
Working in the Client's Home
Conducting a Family Assessment
Developing a Service Plan
Cultural Sensitivity
Empowerment
Advocacy
Substance Abuse
Risk Assessment
Cognitive Restructuring Techniques
Teaching Skills to Families
Stress Management
Parent Training

Training should not be a one-time event, but rather an ongoing activity. The following are issues that must be addressed in developing and institutionalizing an ongoing training capacity for family preservation services:

Who should be trained in addition to the family preservation workers and supervisors (e.g., administrative staff, referring workers, court staff, community agencies)?

Who will provide the training (national organizations, schools of social work, the state training staff, experienced providers)?

How will training be financed (line item in budget; build training costs into direct program operating costs)?

What will the content be? How will ongoing training needs be assessed?

How will the training be evaluated?

Training can be both formal and informal. Informal training occurs during a supervisory conference as the supervisor suggests different ways of looking at a problem or different strategies for helping a family break a destructive pattern of interaction. Staff members should be involved in identifying the kind of ongoing training they need to work effectively with the families and kinds of problems they are experiencing. Formal ongoing training can be supplemented in several ways, some at minimal or no cost. Staff members within the agency may have expertise in a particular area and can give workshops or other presentations on topics such as incest, learning disabilities, or management of anger. Staff members from community agencies may also be willing to conduct workshops on topics of concern in their area of expertise, such as substance abuse. Local therapists might also be enlisted to provide training in methods, techniques, and approaches to working with families.

In addition to formalized training, some agencies have found it very helpful for staff members to build in other kinds of staff supports. For example, allowing time each week for staff members to come together to discuss cases is extremely important. They are able to receive suggestions and guidance from their peers, as well as share their successes. Staff members receive support and encouragement from their peers if they are feeling frustrated or stressed.

Contracting consultation services from an experienced practitioner is another form of support. The consultant can offer a range of services that can assist an individual staff member or the whole staff. For example, the consultant may accompany a particular staff member to a family's home to help assess the family's problems, offer advice on resolving a particular problem, or help deal with a particularly difficult or complex situation. The consultant may also meet with the whole staff on problem cases that can provide a learning experience for everyone. A case is presented by a particular staff member and the consultant leads the discussion, offering observations and raising questions on intervention strategies. The session is informal and staff members are encouraged to express their ideas about the family dynamics and possible ways to intervene.

Selecting a Service Delivery System

Family preservation services are delivered through a wide range of program models. Although the underlying principles of family preservation services are common across programs, program design is quite flexible; no one model has proven more effective than others, and there is room for variability and creativity. The services can be delivered in a variety of agency settings, including child welfare, mental health, juvenile justice, or through an interagency approach. Family crises put children at risk of placement in each of these systems. The family preservation approach to preventing placements has proven adaptable to each of these systems and can provide a framework for interagency collaboration.

Programs are currently operating in public and voluntary child welfare, mental health, and youth service agencies across the country. Some programs accept referrals only from within their own systems. Others have greater flexibility, due to broader legal mandates or greater flexibility of funding sources, and have broadened their target population to include referrals from different systems. For example, family preservation services that have been developed in public social service agencies generally accept referrals only from within their system, primarily from child protection services. Voluntary child welfare agencies, however, may seek funding from social services, mental health, or juvenile justice, and accept referrals from each system.

A family preservation program housed in a community mental health center in Henderson, North Carolina, for example, takes referrals from child protective services and the courts (see Appendix A). A broad legal framework allows this agency to serve a wide variety of clients with mental health problems. Sweetser Children's Home, a residential treatment center with a family preservation component, receives funds from social services, mental health, and juvenile justice, and accepts referrals from several sources (see Appendix A). Interagency agreements may need to be developed that specify how the agencies will work together, including referral procedures, case staffing, case reviews, agency responsibilities, and procedures for resolving any conflicts that may arise.

Family preservation services can be delivered by either a public agency, a voluntary agency, or through a voluntary agency with public funding. Each method has advantages and disadvantages, as well as administrative prerequisites.

Family Preservation Services in a Public Agency

In this category, a local public agency such as a department of social services, a community mental health center, or a youth service agency, is responsible for developing and directly operating the service. Guidelines are generally set by a governing state agency. Staff members are public employees governed by civil service systems.

Advantages. Other services provided by the agency may be drawn upon to benefit family preservation clients. For example, if a family preservation service is housed in a local department of social services, other agency services such as homemaker, parent aide, or day care may be called upon by family preservation staff members. If housed in a community mental health center, the family preservation service staff can draw upon the center's range of services, such as psychiatric or psychological evaluations, consultation, individual or group therapy. Direct operation allows for greater control of the program and furthers the building of a strong philosophical base for a family-centered approach throughout the agency. Although it is often easier to obtain services housed within the same agency, inter-agency agreements can also broaden the range of community services available to family preservation clients.

Public agency staff members have experience in working with client families that would need family preservation services and often have worked in families' homes. Public agency staff members are generally enthusiastic about the opportunity to deliver family preservation services. They have usually been responsible for large caseloads and are often greatly frustrated by having too little time to work directly with families. This situation is particularly frustrating for master's-level social workers eager to use their clinical skills to help clients make changes in their lives. With large caseloads, workers can do little more than respond to crises and perform some case management functions. The small caseloads intrinsic to the family preservation service concept offer public agency workers a chance to use their clinical skills and an opportunity to really make a difference in their client's lives—the reason they became social workers in the first place. Staff turnover is extremely low because morale and satisfaction are high.

Providing this service directly also helps the agency to build a better image in the community. The agency is investing resources in supporting and stabilizing families in the community. Families rapidly spread the word that they were treated respectfully and received the help they needed to stay together. Family preservation projects try to obtain the services of other community agencies, both public and private, to help their families, and through these working relationships a broad spectrum of community agencies experience the positive way that the public agency is helping families. Through this service program, the public agency clearly activates its commitment to family stability. For a local department of social services—the agency that has the legal mandate to remove children from their families—the positive effects of family preservation services may counterbalance some of the negative community feelings aroused by removal of children.

Disadvantages. Civil service regulations about hiring workers and supervisors on the basis of their ranking on a civil service list can limit the choice of staff members most suited for family preservation work. If hired as an exception to the civil service list, they may not be able to receive a permanent title in that position.

Aides may be hired as independent contractors but this frequently means that they do not qualify for health or life insurance or pension plans.

Union and or civil service regulations may not allow for the number of hours family preservation services require, the smaller caseload sizes than other workers, the accumulation of overtime not compensated by money, more vacation or time-off than other staff members, or higher salaries.

Tension may arise among workers with smaller and higher caseloads, adding to the generally low morale.

Public agencies generally have a negative image with the client, as "the people who remove your children."

Public agencies cannot make program and policy changes quickly. Because of their size and bureaucratic nature, changes have to be approved by a number of persons at different levels of the hierarchy. Sometimes approval is not given, and even when it is, it often takes a long time in coming.

Public agencies cannot close intake. They have high staff turnover, staff freezes, and frequent serious case crises—all leading to a tendency to add to workers' caseloads or to pull workers off one assignment for other duties.

Public employees may be discouraged from taking a high visibility or vocal advocacy role. Lobbying is often assigned to, and orchestrated by, staff members other than those engaged in the direct delivery of service.

Administrative prerequisites. Administrative prerequisites include the following:

Ability to pick direct service staff members and supervisors on their ability and willingness to perform the service

Maintenance of low caseload size

Ability to work the necessary number of hours and have the required access to clients

A supportive organizational environment; flexible working hours, adequate time-off, pay differentials

Staff members in leadership positions committed to the provision of family preservation services

Family Preservation Services in a Voluntary Agency

In this model the public agency purchases family preservation services from a voluntary provider [see *Purchasing Family Preservation Services* [1988] for a discussion of purchase methods]. This model also has many advantages and disadvantages. Because voluntary providers are not bound by the civil service system, they have greater flexibility in hiring staff members and in allowing for flexible work schedules that incorporate evening and weekend work hours as well as 24-hour coverage. Also, voluntary agencies that have a good track record in a community will not have to overcome any negative images and therefore can establish trust more quickly with client families.

Public agencies are often underfunded and have difficulty delivering those services that are their mandated responsibility. The development of a new program in a public agency would be a further drain on a management already overtaxed with managing the day-to-day crises in an overburdened system. In this situation it would be more advantageous for the public agency to contract with a voluntary provider to develop and operate the service. To assure an effective partnership, several issues should be resolved before starting a program. To eliminate disputes over the types of cases that are referred, clear criteria should be established for accepting and rejecting cases. Clear procedures should be established for how the agencies will communicate and which levels of staff will be involved in matters concerning policy, case decisions, and contract issues. Monitoring and evaluation procedures should be agreed upon and established in writing. Finally, a method is needed for resolving disputes concerning handling of cases or contract issues.

Advantages. Voluntary agencies under no civil service constraints can be more selective in choosing appropriate staff members. They may draw more job applicants, because employment in private agencies may be viewed by some as more prestigious.

Nonunionized voluntary agencies have more control over working hours, compensation, and compensatory time and vacation allowances.

Costs of providing services are generally less then a public agency would incur for the same services.

The community and clients generally view the voluntary agency more favorably than the public agency.

Voluntary agencies have more freedom to experiment with new service patterns and to make changes and adaptations because the decision-making process is simpler.

Staff members are less apt to be pulled off into other programs.

Voluntary agency employees can participate fully in advocating for legislative, governmental, and social change.

Disadvantages. Some voluntary agencies that wish to deliver family preservation services may have had limited experience with the kinds of client families they will be asked to serve.

The small scale of some programs poses certain problems: insufficient staff to provide back-up in case of unplanned temporary staff loss due to illness or crisis; low or no promotional opportunities for experienced staff members, who may leave.

Agency financing is often fragile. Cash flow problems may occur more frequently. A voluntary agency administrator, who may also be a supervisor, puts substantial time and energy into agency survival issues, leaving less for program issues.

Linkage with the referring public agency may be difficult because the voluntary agency may lack a sophisticated knowledge of how the public system works.

Residential treatment centers that initiate family preservation services are sometimes erroneously suspected of still being interested only in out-of-home care and using family preservation services as a conduit into that program.

Although they are capable of being advocates, some voluntary staff members may feel that their only function is as a practitioner.

Administrative prerequisites. Administrative prerequisites include the following:

A detailed request for proposal and contract that spells out clients to be served, services contracted, terms of payment, and the roles of the state and voluntary provider

Clear criteria and guidelines for case referral, case disposition and the handling of disputes over cases

A system for meetings and communication between contractors and providers

An agreed-upon monitoring and evaluation process for the programs

Licensing criteria that do not contradict but require and support family preservation services

Joint training of referral source and provider agency staff members

Stable funding base for the voluntary agency; ability to calculate costs of service

A governing and advisory board that reflects the community served and the network of service provider colleagues

Deciding whether to use a public or voluntary agency service delivery system should be based on a knowledge of what the program entails, the advantages, disadvantages, and administrative prerequisites of each, and the political realities in each jurisdiction.

Other Administrative Considerations

Financing

Currently, no federal funding stream is specifically targeted to finance family preservation programs. Most states are committing state dollars to fund pilot projects or to begin phasing-in statewide family preservation services.

States are also looking into ways to make better use of existing federal programs to expand services, including family preservation services, for families and children. For example, by maximizing federal financial participation under Title IV-E of the Social Security Act, states can generate additional federal dollars. State dollars being used for foster care maintenance can then be redirected to finance a range of child welfare services, such as family preservation [Center for the Study of Social Policy 1988a]. Potential uses of Medicaid to finance critically needed services for children and their families, such as family preservation, are being examined and piloted by various agencies [Center for the Study of Social Policy 1988c] (see Beacon Counseling Services, Appendix A). In some states, family preservation services are being planned by a consortium of agencies that may include social services, mental health, special education, and juvenile services. Financing strategies involve contributions from each participating agency, which may include funds, staff positions, or support services.

Interagency Collaboration

Family preservation is an effective service approach for any agency authorized to place children in out-of-home care. Most often, the families seen by various service agencies experience similar types of problems, although they may respond to problems in different ways. It is common for a family experiencing multiple difficulties to be involved with or to require services from several agencies simultaneously. To ensure better coordination of services and responsiveness to the needs of the whole family, some family preservation strategies involve the collaboration of multiple agencies such as social services, mental health, juvenile services, and special education. These approaches to collaborative planning and implementation of family preservation services can take various forms and promote change across systems in both the philosophy and practice of serving families.

One model of collaboration involves shared financing among agencies while one agency assumes the responsibility of administration for the program. In Maine, for example, a consortium of agencies including mental health, social services, and juvenile services contributes funds for family preservation services. The funds are administered by the Department of Mental Health, which contracts with providers across the state to deliver family preservation services. Each provider then accepts referrals from any of the consortium agencies. (See Sweetser Children's Home, Appendix A.)

Another collaborative model involves shared financing, as well as shared management and decision-making. A family preservation initiative in Contra Costa, California is financed with shared funds from social services, mental health, probation, and special education. A management group, consisting of representatives of each collaborating agency, takes responsibility for planning and policy development and for examining how family preservation can be the focal point for other areas of collaboration and change beyond financing. For example, agencies are examining their placement standards, the reasons for placement, and how imminent risk is defined. The assessment process is another area for study. What does each agency need to know and why? Can a common assessment instrument be developed that will satisfy the information needs of each agency? If agencies share a common philosophy, value, and service approach, training can become another area of collaboration and shared resources.

The potential for creating greater efficiency, responsiveness, and effectiveness in helping families through interagency approaches to family preservation has only begun to be explored. It is clearly being demonstrated that multiple service systems can agree to the principles and can collaborate to develop a family preservation service project. Emerging, however, are creative uses of family preservation as a starting point and catalyst in promoting the adoption of these principles, values, and methods of working with families within and across systems.

Policy Manuals

Policy manuals for family preservation services should avoid confusing format problems often found in manuals in general. One problem is a failure to separate policy statements from instructions on how to perform the services. Most policy manuals are a combination of organization policy and training. They would be more helpful if policy could be distinguished from process. One way to resolve this is to put policy statements in italics. Another is to have separate sections for policy and process.

The lack of an index and cross-references to other pertinent sections of the manual is the second problem.

Staff members' ignorance of the existence of agency policy is a third problem. The most frequent error here is merely briefing the staff in the family preservation services unit about the policy statements. All organization employees should be involved in understanding how the agency's policies fit with those governing their particular operations.

The final problem is the failure to involve all staff levels and consumers in the drafting of policy.

Family preservation services sections of policy manuals should cover at least the following topics:

> Definition of family preservation services
>
> How they carry out the mission of the organization
>
> Where they fit into the continuum of services in the community and in this organization
>
> What client populations are served
>
> What families are eligible
>
> How referrals are made
>
> Essential components of service
>
> Obtaining financial assistance and other services
>
> Purchase of service

Systems Advocacy

The job description of a family preservation service contains four principal categories of tasks:

> Dealing with intrapersonal and interpersonal problems
>
> Teaching skills and knowledge
>
> Linking clients with community resources and services
>
> Advocating for broader societal reforms that will bene-fit families

Most agencies and staff members struggle to provide the first three categories of help. The fourth is almost universally neglected or at best underdeveloped. The average staff member finds it exhausting to deal with the typical bureaucracy for his or her clients, and depressing to think of all the families that must deal with these institutions without an advocate. Too many voluntary and public agencies do not have a clear mission statement, or a process devoted to social action. When it comes time to collect the energy needed for social action, most feel that they expended their energy and served a useful purpose in giving direct service.

There are two major impediments to social action on the part of family preservation services: seeing this as a legitimate activity for a practitioner, and knowing what to do and how to do it. Other types of practitioners engaged in family preservation may not have any social action orientation in their professional discipline, as the tenets of social work do. Staff job descriptions, hiring interviews, and the selection process should all include the expectation for some form of social action.

The following are key tasks for the administrator:

Appointing someone to oversee the program's overall advocacy strategy

Including social action in the mission statement

Setting yearly objectives and evaluating them

Examples of social action include:

Staff questioning of political candidates on their position on issues supporting families

Becoming politically active in campaigns

Forming local and state coalitions with others who can promote the agency's cause

Participating in the social action committee of professional and civic organizations

Giving financial support to the advocacy activities of national organizations

Educating the public via press releases and stories, radio and TV talk shows, conferences, studies, and surveys

Giving expert testimony at legislative hearings

Creating demonstration projects

Petitioning directly for changes

Linking with state child advocacy organizations

Preparing the Professional and Lay Communities

Agencies serving families and children frequently feel that they lack the understanding and support of the community for the work they do. The most tangible effect of these deficits is insufficient resources to do the job and a negative climate of opinion toward the notion of keeping certain families together.

More specifically, family preservation services often struggle to keep family members together whom the community would just as soon see apart. The community consists of both the lay public at large and the professional community that serves the same families; ignorance of family preservation services and negative attitudes toward certain families are unfortunately not restricted to the lay community—professional colleagues sometimes feel the same way. Those initiating family preservation services have to educate the community about the problems and needs of families and the role family preservation services play; obtain support for the purposes of the program; and elicit the additional professional and programmatic assistance families will need.

The distance between helping organizations and the community continues when the information about what families need is possessed by the organization alone. The first tasks, then, are education and involvement. Nebraska approached this problem by hiring community organizers who went into areas where family preservation services were most likely to be needed. The organizers were identified by members of the lay and professional communities. People were asked to join a task force that would study the needs of families in crisis in their community. Information was gathered that would form a picture of what the community needed. Statistics were developed from available data. Powerful testimony was provided by families who had been or were in trouble and without help.

This strategy resulted in a better understanding of the needs of individual families and the gaps in the array of services. The need for family preservation services was recognized by the group as a whole. The process of joint study resulted in joint ownership of a plan for services and a broad-based commitment to achieving it. Other states have planned community involvement as a desirable way to begin programs.

Lay and professional community members should be kept involved once programs have begun. Using community representatives only for a needs assessment is a common error. A continuing relationship can be achieved through their membership on a steering or advisory committee for the program.

Developing an Advisory Board

Some family preservation projects have found it helps to develop an advisory board composed of representatives of local agencies that may interact with the project and also provide service to the project's clients. Advisory boards for family preservation services are generally composed of the following:

Professionals from agencies most likely to refer families, such as courts, departments of social services, mental health organizations, and services for developmental disabilities, education, juvenile justice, drug and alcohol abuse

Members of the parent agency board and staff

Child and family advocates

Representatives of churches, voluntary agencies

Policy decisionmakers

Gaining community support for the family preservation program is a major purpose in developing the board. Enlisting the participation of other community agencies in establishing the program and developing policy helps to ensure their continuing involvement and support. Developing procedures for joint referrals and interagency collaboration is a less formidable endeavor if done through an advisory board that is already invested in the program. Any problems that may occur in daily operations when relating to community agencies can, if necessary, be brought to the board for assistance in their resolution.

Another important function of the board can be advocacy at the systems level. Family preservation staff members will be able to identify problems and trends affecting families that require a broad-based community-level approach for resolution. Lack of affordable housing, teen pregnancy, substance abuse in schools, and increasing reports of child abuse, are examples of problems that cannot be solved by any one agency, but rather require a coordinated community-based response. The advisory board is in an excellent position to become the catalyst for promoting social change in any of these areas.

The following are benefits of an advisory board:

Better communication and understanding among the helping systems present

More appropriate referrals

Ideas for program change

Case management for families known to all the systems

Monitoring of the program's progress

Act as a political force committed to and knowledgeable about family preservation services and family issues

Good public relations for the family preservation services program among the professional and private groups the members influence

Costs of an advisory board may include the following:

Small out-of-pocket expenditures for refreshments and materials

Moderate to high cost in time to carry out and follow up on committee recommendations

Integrating Family Preservation Services in an Agency

Change is difficult, whether personal or organizational. The addition of family preservation services in an agency may introduce changes in philosophy, personnel, and organizational structure. Existing staff members may feel threatened and resist the changes that have to take place. They may view the new program as infringing on their turf and feel resentful of the attention that the new program may be receiving from administration, other community agencies, and possibly the media. Some of this initial skepticism or resistance can be expected, and is inherent in the process of change. A deliberate effort by the administration to include staff members in the planning and integrating of the service into the agency will reduce the negativity and gain acceptance for family preservation services more quickly. The administration can take the following steps to prepare the organization for change:

1.   *Ensure that all staff members have the opportunity to incorporate the philosophy and values of family preservation services.*

This may mean taking time at staff meetings, or bringing in consultants or trainers to work with the staff on values regarding families. Particularly for staff members who have worked primarily with children, it is important to stress that the best interests of the child are paramount in family preservation programs. Working to strengthen a family to ensure that it is capable of providing nurturance, protection, and a loving, healthy environment for a child is in the best interests of the child.

2. *Provide opportunities for the staff to become educated about family preservation services.*

The staff should have a good understanding of how family preservation programs operate. This can be done by sharing written materials on family preservation or showing films that have been developed by some projects. If finances allow, staff members from various agencies can be brought in to describe their family preservation programs. Also, various national and regional conferences may include presentations on family preservation programs that staff members might attend.

3. *Include staff members in all stages of planning.*

Staff representatives should be involved in all planning meetings and discussions about program design and operations. They will make significant contributions to the ways in which the new service can best be linked with other parts of the agency in the least disruptive way.

4. *Include other agency staff members in the training of the family preservations staff.*

This will allow other agency staff members to be better grounded in the philosophy, and to gain a better appreciation for the complexity and effectiveness, of this work.

Special Considerations

Public social service agencies.   If family preservation services are to be developed in a public social service agency, consideration should be given to how this service will relate to existing protective services and family service programs.

Where to place the new service in the agency will be one of the initial decisions. If most of the referrals are expected to come from protective services, agencies may choose to house the family preservation service within protective services. This will build relationships between the two service staffs, thereby reducing such problems as referring inappropriate cases or withholding referrals. Some agencies, however, prefer to house family preservation services in a family services division regardless of the source of referrals. This is partly a symbolic measure to highlight for the community the fact that family preservation staff members are not the same as investigation staff members, and are not responsible for removing children from their homes.

Other considerations will revolve around how staff members from the various programs will be involved in case identification, referral, and selection procedures. For example, some agencies have established screening teams to review cases referred to family preservation services and determine whether they are appropriate. Usually the team will include supervisors from the referring units such as protective services and family services, as well as the family preservation supervisor. Supervisors can then discuss why a particular case does or does not meet eligibility criteria, and jointly reach a decision. This process eliminates the bad feelings that can be generated when cases are rejected and sent back to a referring unit without fully explaining the rationale for the rejection.

Residential treatment centers. Some residential treatment centers have expanded their mission to include prevention of out-of-home placement and have incorporated family preservation services into their program. Once the agency makes a commitment to preserving families, this philosophy should become incorporated into all agency service programs. The staff members of the treatment center should share the commitment to work with families so that they will effectively coordinate their work with that of the family preservation staff. Again, it is most helpful to involve the residential treatment staff in planning for a family preservation component to ensure good working relationships between the two services. A description of a successful model of this type, Sweetser Children's Home, is found in Appendix A.

Community mental health centers. Family preservation programs are also being developed in community mental health centers. One advantage of this setting is its easy access to the range of mental health services offered by the center. Also the center's mandate to serve a catchment area enables a broad target population to be included as appropriate for the service. The target population, for example, could be referrals from social services, the courts, mental health agencies, youth service agencies, or even self-referrals. A successful center model has been developed in North Carolina (see Appendix A).

References

Center for the Study of Social Policy. *Claiming Available Federal Funds Under Title IV-E of the Social Security Act*. Washington, DC: Center for the Study of Social Policy, 1988a.

Center for the Study of Social Policy. *Purchasing Family Preservation Services: Methods of Payment that Encourage High Quality Programs*. Washington, DC: Center for the Study of Social Policy, 1988b.

Center for the Study of Social Policy. *Use of Medicaid to Support Community-Based Services to Children and Families*. Washington, DC: Center for the Study of Social Policy, 1988c.

5

Evaluation

Summary of Pertinent Research

S tates that have adopted a family preservation perspective have established special programs for families at the brink of disruption due to abuse, neglect, emotional or mental illness, or delinquency. The unifying theme for these programs has been a conceptual base grounded in family therapy and systems theories, with most of the services provided in the homes of high-risk families.

Most of the research on family preservation programs is rather fugitive: the results are published as part of project summaries for grants, as monographs with limited circulation, or as mimeographed internal reports, but are available upon request. The following summary profiles research on several family preservation programs. Additional studies of family preservation programs and less intensive service models with similar objectives are cited in the bibliography. This summary is not meant to be an exhaustive review of the literature, but rather an overview of the most widely circulated reports on the effectiveness of these programs.

Homebuilders

Perhaps the best known of all the family preservation programs, Homebuilders began in Tacoma, Washington, in 1974. Behavioral Sciences Institute now operates Homebuilders programs in eight counties in Washington state and will expand to four more counties in the state by the end of 1991.

The program serves children and families with presenting problems of abuse, neglect, incorrigibility, family conflict, mental illness, delinquency, developmental disabilities, and addictions. Almost all the work takes place in the family's usual environment, where the problems generally occur. Each family receives a tailored treatment plan and intervention by professionally trained counselors and social workers. One Homebuilders practitioner provides treatment to two families at a time and may offer sophisticated psychotherapeutic treatment as well as advocacy and help in obtaining material resources (e.g., rent money, emergency food or housing, medical care). Clients are directly involved in identifying problems and developing skills and strategies to resolve them.

The Homebuilders programs accept only families at risk of imminent disruption, yet report very high "success" rates (i.e., rate of children remaining with their families). In an early report, Kinney et al. [1977] described the first years of the Homebuilders program and reported a success rate of over 90%, that is, only 13 of 134 children at risk were placed. From 1974 to 1988, the program served 4,194 children at risk of placement. A subgroup of 678 Homebuilders client children who were status offenders targeted for out-of-home care was served from 1982 to 1986. At 12 months after Homebuilders service intake, 592 (87%) of these children avoided out-of-home placement [Haapala and Kinney 1988]. (Note: These figures reflect *children* who remained home, not *families* who avoided disruption. If a given family had two children at risk of placement, and only one was placed, the "success" rate would be 50% for children and 0% for the family.)

In 1987, Behavioral Sciences Institute began a Homebuilders program in the Bronx, New York. The program receives referrals of victims of child abuse and neglect, Persons in Need of Supervision (PINS), and juvenile delinquents. The Edna McConnell Clark Foundation supplied some initial financial support; the ongoing funding contract is with the Human Resources Administration, New York City.

Other states (e.g., California, New Jersey, Michigan) have established similar programs, often using staff members from the Behavioral Sciences Institute for on-site training and/or to provide "apprenticeships" with the original Homebuilders program in the state of Washington. All such programs share the basic parameters of short-term (four to six weeks), intensive (15 to 25 hours per week) interventions to respond to a crisis that would likely result in placement.

University of Utah

The University of Utah Social Research Institute at the Graduate School of Social Work and Behavioral Sciences Institute recently completed a major study [Fraser et al. 1988] evaluating the Homebuilders program and comparing it to a somewhat similar program in Utah. This study examined outcomes for 453 families and included a 12-month follow-up for 263 of the families and 342 children. Rigorous definitions were used. "Placement" included two weeks or longer in shelter care, detention, psychiatric hospitalization, runaways, and living with friends, as well as foster or group care. Overall, 71.3% of the families remained intact. The 12-month follow-up showed that 66.3% of the Homebuilders families (71.4% of the children) remained together, while 56.6% of the Utah families (61.9% of the children) had no episodes of placement during the year. Successful cases also received significantly improved ratings on measures of school adjustment, delinquent behavior, behavior at home, parenting and supervision of both younger and older children, parental knowledge about child care, and parental attitudes toward placement.

Families First

The University of California, Davis, evaluated an intensive four to six-week treatment program for abusive families developed by Families First of Davis. Practitioners carried two cases each. The study used a wait-list comparison group, that is, families referred for whom no practitioner was available were followed to compare their outcomes with the treated group. At the end of one year, preliminary results for 50 families showed almost twice as many children in the comparison group were in out-of-home placements (51% vs. 26% of the children in the treatment group) [Barton et al. n.d.].

Intensive Family Services

The Maryland Department of Human Resources, Social Services Administration, initiated the Intensive Family Services (IFS) project in 1984, using public employees rather than purchase-of-service. The project works with families of children at risk of placement, and uses teams of one worker and one aide, with a caseload of six families. The length of service is limited to 90 days, and services include frequent home visits and flexible funds to purchase either additional services or basic necessities such as food, clothing, and shelter. Workers are trained in family systems and family therapy. Families receive on average about 3.5 contacts per week from one of the workers, with roughly 40% of all contacts provided in-home, and the remainder being phone or collateral contacts [Pearson et al. 1987].

Evaluation data from a 1984 pilot project showed only 10% of the families experienced placement, and that the counties that had the IFS project available demonstrated a substantially greater decline in foster care intake than non-IFS counties.

A larger-scale evaluation study covering May 1985 through November 1986 compared families receiving IFS to families receiving traditional protective service casework, and documented significantly fewer placements as well as significant decreases on measures of risk to the child.

Hennepin County, Minnesota

The Hennepin County Community Services Department (Child Welfare Division) established five special home-based service units in January 1986. A pilot program, begun in August 1985, was evaluated by the Center for the Study of Youth Policy at the University of Minnesota [AuClaire and Schwartz 1986].

Teams of two workers were assigned four families, with an average length of treatment of 37 days. The model drew from both structural family therapy and cognitive/behavioral approaches. The project was targeted to adolescents, age 12 to 17. Families were eligible for the study if they had already been approved for placement by both a supervisor and a program manager. (Youths who were court-ordered to placement were excluded, as were youths in state custody.) If the home-based service unit had a space available, the adolescent most recently approved for placement but not yet placed was assigned to the treatment group. A comparison group was constructed by randomly selecting adolescents who would have been eligible for the home-based project, but for whom no opening existed at the time of approval for placement.

This procedure, as well as the method of analysis, is conservative for two reasons: (1) by the time an adolescent has been approved for placement at several levels, all concerned are likely to have become set on the placement plan, including the parents (who often are the initiators of placement requests for this age group); and (2) the authors included all families referred for home-based services, even if the family refused services or withdrew shortly after their beginning.

Although the groups did not differ significantly on the incidence of placement, the home-based services group used 21% of "available placement days," vs. 32% for the comparison group. When shelter or respite placements are excluded, the treatment group used only half as many placement days (15% vs. 30%). Moreover, the placements for the treatment group were less restrictive and more likely to be evaluated as successful by the staff of the placement agency [AuClaire and Schwartz 1986].

California

The California legislature enacted a bill in 1984 to fund eight intensive in-home services demonstration projects in preventing foster care placement. Findings from a two-year interim report from a three-year study currently under way by Walter McDonald Associates indicate that out of 538 children who were followed up six months after termination of service, 84% did not experience a placement. The study observed that children who had been adjudicated dependent or have experienced previous placements were more likely to be placed than children without such histories. Children with disabilities and/or who were performing below grade level were also found more likely to be placed.

In comparing data from the Child Well-Being Scales for families that experienced a child placement and families for which placement did not occur, the following hypothesis was proposed:

> Placement decisions are related to four areas of concern by workers: the ability of a family to recognize its problems, cooperate with caregivers, and be motivated to solve problems; the availability and accessibility of resources; parental disposition, especially with regard to disciplining children; and the availability of a habitable residence. [Yuan and McDonald 1988]

Systemic Crisis Intervention Program

The Houston, Texas, Child Guidance Center Systemic Crisis Intervention Program (SCIP) differs from many of the other programs reviewed here in that the target population comprises suicidal and seriously disturbed youths. The SCIP model was designed to provide an alternative to psychiatric hospitalization for children and adolescents [Gutstein and Rudd 1987; Gutstein et al. 1987].

SCIP uses a four-to-six member multidisciplinary team to intervene at the point of a crisis with the potential for hospitalization, such as a suicide attempt or threat or other self-destructive behavior; escalating drug or alcohol use; homicide threat or attempt; or extreme withdrawal and depression. For a typical case, the team provides: *(1)* a two-hour evaluation session to determine the patient's danger to self and others, as well as the family's ability and willingness to make use of the program; *(2)* six to eight one-hour preparation sessions with the individual family members; and *(3)* two four-hour extended family gatherings during the crisis period. Most families are referred for ongoing therapy following the crisis.

The theoretical framework appears to be a modification of networking interventions with borrowing from multiple impact therapy and family systems theory. In brief, the intervention uses the crisis as an opportunity to strengthen the family's natural support network by accomplishing a reconciliation with split-off elements of the network. The intervention also tries to block extreme, polarizing reactions to the crisis by offering the family enough support and sense of safety that they can tolerate the upheaval (e.g., the program may provide a short-term hospital stay if necessary, or day treatment, or respite care). But all interventions focus on building the family's own capacity for dealing with the problem.

Ratings on five measures were completed for a total of 83 patients at the end of treatment and at follow-up intervals of three, six, 12, and 18 months. Measures included severity of presenting problems, family and marital functioning, number of problem episodes, and adaptive behavior ratings. All five measures resulted in significant improvement, which was sustained through the follow-up periods. A total of five hospitalizations or residential placements took place among the 83 patients during the whole follow-up period.

Planning an Evaluation

This section reexamines the literature summarized above as a means of considering the issues that should ideally be considered in evaluating family preservation services. It is important to note that not all of these issues can ever be dealt with completely, given practical and ethical constraints imposed by the real world of service delivery.

Planning evaluation research projects can be seen as a process of clarifying expectations, choosing approaches for gathering evidence on whether the program attained specified outcomes, and anticipating problems in interpreting the evidence. The existing research on family preservation programs is an excellent beginning, but the evidence is open to many other explanations.

Since evaluation research is a means of gathering facts to guide decision-making, its usefulness rests on the quality of the evidence that results from the effort, which in turn depends on eliminating as much ambiguity as possible from the findings. The evaluator aims to document the effects of the intervention, and to rule out other possible explanations for those effects. Ideally, the evaluator also hopes to discover ways to fine-tune the intervention by determining the key factors in success.

When new treatment approaches are developed, initial evaluations are usually fairly straightforward and descriptive, documenting in some measurable way the improvement in people receiving the new intervention. As the intervention gains acceptance, the early evaluations are often challenged on grounds that the effectiveness of the intervention was not adequately proven because the research was not sufficiently sophisticated or controlled to rule out other explanations for positive results.

Other critics may accept the early research, while calling for study of more sophisticated questions. Is the new intervention more effective then the more traditional interventions? What clients are most likely to benefit from the intervention? What about long-term effects? Can the intervention be replicated with equally positive results in other places, with other populations, with different kinds of staffing? What are the critical components of the intervention? Are there potentially negative effects, and if so, what clients are most vulnerable to them?

Defining Interventions Clearly

Rather dramatic claims have been made for the effectiveness of family-based services in avoiding out-of-home placement. Unfortunately, the actual interventions are often not rigorously defined, so that comparisons among programs are difficult if not impossible. At a minimum, the following parameters should be spelled out:

1. *Intensity.*

Programs designed to keep families together and prevent unnecessary foster care vary widely in the intensity of the service provided—the number and length of contacts at various points in the delivery of the service.

2. *Duration.*

Similarly, programs vary widely in the duration of services—the length of time the program remains involved with the family.

3. *Caseloads.*

Related to both intensity and duration is the size of the caseload carried by each staff member. The addition of other team members in the assessment and treatment process may lead to a slight increase in caseload.

4. *Staff qualifications.*

Programs have used staff members with social work degrees (both bachelor and master degrees), psychology degrees, and no special degrees. Some require rigorous preservice and inservice training, including an internship, others ask for little special training. A team may be composed of a professional practitioner and a paraprofessional parent aide, or two professionally trained copractitioners.

5. *Intervention models.*

Although virtually all family preservation models share a focus on treating the entire family, they differ greatly in the theoretical perspectives that undergird the interventions, at least as described in published reports about the programs.

Some adopt a cognitive/behavioral approach, emphasizing techniques drawn from social learning theory (e.g., behavioral contracting, cognitive restructuring, stress management). Many draw from various schools of family systems approaches, using techniques such as restructuring, boundary-making, genograms, eco-maps, renetworking. Others do not identify a particular approach, hiring staff members who have at least some history of working with families from whatever perspective, and so have a hodgepodge of methods, depending on the preferences of the individual staff member.

Issues for Evaluation of Intervention

Failing to clearly delineate the characteristics of the intervention greatly limits the usefulness of evaluation research. Forsythe [1987] notes that many program developers make choices in designing new programs without clearly understanding the variety of choices and the cost and practice implications of each. Evaluations that clearly define the intervention under study can offer critical guidance to program developers by providing information about these issues.

In designing an evaluation, the researcher should build in methods for collecting data about the intervention itself. This includes a description of the workers' intervention theory (i.e., how do they explain what they do—what theoretical framework do they use in understanding families and in choosing intervention strategies?); as well as documentation of the interventions actually attempted, their frequency and duration. Some examples of data collection instruments that capture such data can be seen in AuClaire and Schwartz [1986]; Pecora et al. [1987]; and Landsman et al. [1985].

Target Populations

Defining the Population

Who are the clients of family preservation programs? By their very nature, the programs target families of children at risk of out-of-home placement. The definition of risk varies, however, depending on how imminent the placement is. For example, some evaluations have included cases where a child is already on the list, waiting for a placement resource to become available. Others include any family that a practitioner identifies as having serious problems, which would result in placement eventually if no improvements are made. In others, the parents, the referring worker, and the program practitioner must all agree that placement is imminent (i.e., very likely to occur within a specified time period such as 48 hours). Perception of risk is also relative to the agency, its resources, caseload size, and so forth. An agency with few resources and a large caseload may draw the line at a higher level of risk.

In addition to the risk-of-placement dimension, programs vary in the types of presenting problems and/or characteristics of the families served. Some programs seem to rule out certain presenting problems, such as families with chronic alcoholism or drug addiction, psychosis, previous placements, and/or families with a weak motivation for help. Other programs do not set any hard-and-fast exclusion criteria, preferring to meet with the family for several sessions to assess whether the service will be helpful or not.

Evaluations should summarize the associated problems faced by the project's families and the progress made in overcoming these problems by the termination of the project. Many programs, for example, use a problem checklist with each family at the assessment and again at termination. It is important to know whether and what change occurred as a result of the service, although the length of time that improvement is sustained and retained is the sounder research measure.

The demographic and socioeconomic characteristics of the children and families served should also be reported in the evaluation. The most commonly reported characteristics include:

> Age, race, and sex of family members
> Family composition
> Income—source and amount
> Employment status
> Education
> Placement history of children
> Reason for removal in previous placements

Issues for Evaluation of Population

Again, evaluation data are most useful when they provide guidelines for program decisions, and when they can be combined with data from similar evaluations to guide broader policy. Failure to describe clearly the target population prevents policy makers from drawing appropriate conclusions about the study.

Outcome Measures

Avoidance of Placement

Given the nature of family preservation services, it is not surprising that the most common measure of program effectiveness is the percentage of children who had been identified as at risk of placement who remain in their homes following the intervention. Statistics on a program's success rate are used to convince legislators to fund and expand the program, as the figures can be easily translated into rough cost savings. This approach has several serious problems, however.

As noted above, the extent to which a child is actually at risk of placement is a matter of subjective judgment. Thus, two programs that claim a placement avoidance rate of 80% may be treating families for whom the risk of placement is very different. Moreover, some programs calculate the rate based on families (i.e., what proportion of treated families had a child placed), and others base their rates on children (i.e., what proportion of children at risk are actually placed). These can be two quite different rates, and may explain some of the discrepancies across different studies of the same program. Information on both rates should be provided.

A third methodological problem lies in the extent to which studies vary both in the length of follow-up time and in the definition of out-of-home placement. Reporting the percentage of children who remain at home at termination of intensive services can be greatly misleading. The protective issues that are placing the child at risk of placement are usually manageable during the time the intensive services are actually being offered, and the public agency charged with protective responsibilities is likely to feel fairly comfortable with leaving a child in the home if the agency knows there will be frequent at-home contacts with a skilled practitioner. Given the episodic nature of crises in the lives of dysfunctional families, however, even a three-month follow-up is likely to underestimate the number of children who will require placement.

Moreover, global reports of placement avoidance fail to discriminate among types of placements. Some programs build in short-term out-of-home respite care, which is not counted as placement, while others count a short stay in a shelter facility as a failure.

But perhaps the most serious flaws in relying on percentage of placement as the main measure of success are conceptual and practical. Out-of-home care or treatment is itself an intervention, with the goals of protecting, healing, and/or rehabilitating the child. The key evaluation question, therefore, is whether intensive home-based interventions that keep children in their own homes are more or less effective than out-of-home care in accomplishing these same objectives. As Kinney has pointed out, if the purpose is only to prevent placements, we could accomplish that quite easily by decreasing placement resources. (In fact, availability of placements, along with parental attitude toward placement, are probably the two best predictors for placement decisions.)

Conceptually, evaluation should be useful in suggesting ways to improve services for those families who otherwise could have been kept together, while identifying key factors that represent such high risk that placement is necessary. In addition, some children who should be placed are not, as indicated by subsequent serious injury or other exacerbation of the presenting problem. The challenge, therefore, is to bring together the developing literature on risk assessment/risk management and family preservation.

Finally, the research by AuClaire and Schwartz [1986] suggests that intensive services are beneficial even when placement is not avoided. Their data demonstrated that children who experienced placement and whose families received intensive services before their placements, were placed in less restrictive environments, for a shorter period of time, and with more positive outcomes than a control group of other children experiencing placement. All of these considerations are masked by the overreliance on avoidance of placement as the primary measure of program success.

Other Outcome Measures

Fortunately, most formal evaluations include other measures of program effectiveness. Most of these can be grouped under four major categories: family functioning, risk to the child, child behavior, and social support. The following are typical instruments:

Family functioning measures typically focus on changes in the family's ability to adapt to stress and change, and on the affective relationships among the members.

Risk measures track change in degree of risk of physical, emotional, and sexual abuse, or neglect.

Child behavior scales measure change in the severity and frequency of disturbed behavior.

Social support scales measure family members' perception of the availability and usefulness of the support provided to them by the central persons in their social network.

Issues for Evaluation of Outcome

As designs for outcome studies have become more sophisticated, researchers are using a more comprehensive approach to measurement. The advantage of multiple measures of program outcome is that the weaknesses of any one measure are balanced out by the strengths of other measures. This becomes a disadvantage if researchers use instruments in a shotgun fashion, that is, without clear conceptual links to the objectives of the intervention.

Perhaps the most serious flaw in the current approaches to these instruments is the failure to control for the bias and reactivity of the measurement process. In most of the available studies, the instruments are completed by the practitioners and the families themselves. Given the often intense relationships formed between them, it is not surprising that evaluations by the participants of either client progress or practitioner helpfulness are treated with skepticism by most critics [Gurman and Kniskern 1981; Bergin and Garfield 1978].

Ideally, an evaluation should triangulate measurement of outcome. That is, multiple measures should be used, from multiple perspectives, so as to reduce the ambiguity of data drawn from any one source or procedure. Practically, this is rarely possible, except in well-funded, sophisticated research. With the advent of more reliable and valid measures, however, even small-scale projects should be able to collect and analyze data on the key variables listed above (see Magura and Moses [1986] for an excellent summary of available instruments pertinent to children's services). If possible, data should be collected from several sources, including, for example, the referring worker, school personnel, the home-based practitioner, and the family members themselves.

The studies summarized above vary greatly in the extent of follow-up outcome data available, which tend to be limited to placement status, a measure that of course retains all the limitations described earlier. In addition to tracking placement status, critical questions for follow-up studies include the incidence of abuse and neglect; physical, mental, and emotional development of children left with their families after having received home-based services; and overall well-being of the children.

Cost Effectiveness

Almost every published report on home-based services refers to the cost savings obtained by keeping children in their own homes, and some attempts at developing a reliable methodology for calculating the savings have been made [see, for example, Haugaard and Hokanson 1983]. Although these illustrations are no doubt necessary as tools to convince budget analysts and legislators to invest in family preservation, caution should be exercised in making claims.

There can be little doubt that child abuse and neglect remain underreported. If we do a better job of encouraging and validating complaints, the potential pool for out-of-home care will continue to increase. Even if we are successful in preventing unnecessary placements, the total number of children in placement may still rise. Moreover, the children who do require out-of-home care are likely to come from families that do not benefit from placement prevention services, that is, they are likely to be the most damaged and thus the most difficult to care for. Their placements will be longer and more costly.

It has been suggested that public child welfare agencies project their placement rates and costs under two assumptions: assuming no increased efforts in placement prevention, and assuming a specific level of increased effort. The agency could then negotiate the flexibility to use placement funds for home-based services to prevent placement, within a cap set by the first method of projecting costs.

Perhaps most convincing are the studies that show overall decreases in expenditures for placement in geographic areas that have home-based services [e.g., Heffner 1985]. In large states, contiguous counties with similar demographic and socioeconomic characteristics could be matched and compared for expenditures over time, with some counties using home-based services and others relying on traditional approaches. Placement trends can be compared in the same county over time, both before and after family preservation services have been implemented.

Issues for Evaluation of Cost Effectiveness

The studies reviewed demonstrate the wide range of parameters used in home-based services. The variables of caseload size, length of treatment, intensity of service, and staffing patterns clearly have significant implications for cost effectiveness. These are the program design issues that make rigorous evaluation so important. At this stage of development, the existing evidence on effectiveness is not refined enough to exclude any model on cost difference alone.

Summary and Conclusions

Home-based family preservation services as a key strategy in avoiding out-of-home placement are well accepted. Many states have at least one home-based service initiative, and some states have truly statewide initiatives.

On the one hand, if these services are to survive and become an established component of services for families, we must avoid the pitfalls of overselling or exaggerating their effectiveness. If the expectations of legislators, budget officers, and taxpayers are raised to unrealistic levels, the credibility of family preservation services will be needlessly damaged. On the other hand, as more states and counties seek to redesign and implement home-based services, they have little critical literature to guide their choices: a quick review of published reports would suggest that virtually every model is very successful at preventing placement, with success rates of 75% to 94%.

Fortunately, much more rigorous evaluations are currently under way. The comparison of Homebuilders and the Utah Family Preservation Services programs [Fraser et al. 1988], research initiated by the New Jersey Department of Youth and Family Services [Feldman 1987], and a multisite evaluation of placement prevention services in California, are all signs of a maturing of research in this arena. In addition, the recent formation of a network of researchers should facilitate the development of a more standardized research protocol, which will give comparison studies more validity. Finally, the continued support of research and program development at the national level by the Children's Bureau of the U.S. Department of Health and Human Services and by the Edna McConnell Clark Foundation are encouraging signs that the field will increasingly base decisions on empirical evidence of effectiveness.

References

AuClaire P., and Schwartz, I.M. *An Evaluation of the Effectiveness of Intensive Home-Based Services as an Alternative to Placement for Adolescents and Their Families*. Minneapolis, MN: Hennepin County Community Services Department, and the University of Minnesota, Hubert H. Humphrey Institute of Public Affairs, 1986.

Barton, Keith; Wood, Sally; Schroeder, Carroll; and Campbell, Jeanne. *In-Home Treatment of Abusive Families*. Davis, CA: Department of Applied Behavioral Sciences, Community Studies & Development, Human Development and Family Studies, University of California, Davis, n.d.

Bergin, Allen E., and Garfield, Sol L., eds. *Handbook of Psychotherapy and Behavior Change* (2d ed.). New York: Wiley, 1978.

Feldman, Leonard. *Evaluating Family-Based Service Programs within an Ecological Context*. Trenton, NJ: Bureau of Research, Evaluation and Quality Assurance, New Jersey Division of Youth and Family Services, 1987.

Forsythe, Peter. "Making Family Centered Services Work: A Report of Family Preservation Projects." Teleconference transcript of the National Child Welfare Resource Center for Management and Administration, June 30, 1987.

Fraser, M.; Pecora, P.; and Haapala, D. *Families in Crisis: Final Report on the Family-Based Intensive Treatment Program*. Salt Lake City, UT: University of Utah, Social Research Institute, 1988.

Gurman, Alan S., and Kniskern, David P. *Family Therapy Outcome Research: Knowns and Unknowns*. Handbook of Family Therapy. New York: Brunner Mazel, 1981.

Gutstein, Steven E.; Rudd, M. David; Graham, J. Christopher; and Rayba, Linda. *Systemic Crisis Intervention as an Alternative to Adolescent Psychiatric Hospitalization: An Outcome Study*. Austin, TX: Hogg Foundation for Mental Health, University of Texas, 1987.

Gutstein, Steven E., and Rudd, David M. *Outcome of Outpatient Family Crisis Intervention with Suicidal Youth.* Houston, TX: Systemic Crisis Intervention Program, Houston Child Guidance Center, 1987.

Haapala, D., and Kinney, J. "Avoiding Out-of-Home Placement of High-Risk Status Offenders Through the Use of Intensive Home-Based Family Preservation Services." *Criminal Justice and Behavior* 15 (1988): 334-348.

Heffner, Gary J. *Family Preservation Services Project in Columbia, GA.* Martinez, GA: Georgia Department of Human Resources, 1985.

Haugaard, J., and Hokanson, B. *Measuring the Cost Effectiveness of Family-Based Services and Out-of-Home Care.* Prepared for the Maryland Department of Human Resources. Oakdale, IA: Institute on Urban and Regional Research, and the National Resource Center on Family-Based Services, 1983.

Kinney, J.M.; Madsen, B.; Fleming, T.; and Haapala, D.A. "Homebuilders: Keeping Families Together." *Journal of Consulting and Clinical Psychology* 43, 4 (1977): 667–673.

Landsman, M.T.; Leung, P.; and Hutchinson, J.R. *Preventive Services to Families in Four States: Subcontractor's Final Report.* Iowa City, IA: National Resource Center on Family-Based Services, 1985.

Magura, Stephen, and Moses, Beth. *Outcome Measures for Child Welfare Services: Theory and Applications.* New York: Child Welfare League of America, 1986.

Pearson, C.L.; Masnyk, K.; and King, P. *Intensive Family Services: Preliminary Evaluation Report.* Baltimore, MD: Maryland Department of Human Resources, 1987.

Pecora, P.J.; Fraser, M.W.; Haapala, D.; and Bartlomé, J.A. *Defining Family Preservation Services: Three Intensive Home-Based Treatment Programs.* Salt Lake City, UT: Research Report Number 1 from the Family-Based Intensive Treatment Project, University of Utah, Graduate School of Social Work, Social Research Institute, 1987.

Yuan, Ying-Ying T., and McDonald, Walter. *Evaluation of AB 62 Demonstration Projects: Year Two Interim Report.* Sacramento, CA: Walter McDonald and Associates, 1988.

Appendices

Appendix A—Organizational Examples

The following summaries include family preservation programs that received funding from the Edna McConnell Clark Foundation. They have been included to illustrate how these services can operate in different settings. The programs (in order of inclusion) are: Beacon Counseling, Inc.; Behavioral Sciences Institute; Centers for New Horizons; Commonweal Family Consulting Services; Home Education Livelihood Program; Kingsley House; Family Preservation Project; Sweetser Children's Home; and Youth Service, Inc.

Beacon Counseling, Inc.
FAMILY PRESERVATION SERVICES
15 WORCESTER STREET
BOSTON, MASSACHUSETTS 02118
(617) 536-6477

History and Background

Beacon Counseling, Inc., formed in 1975, is a voluntary, not-for-profit mental health counseling, education, and consultation agency. Family Preservation Services and the Family Project are current home-based, outreach family preservation services providing brief, in-home, crisis intervention services to families on the verge of having one or more children placed outside the home. After 30 days of crisis intervention services, families can receive longer-term, weekly in-home family counseling and may join the Parent Partnership Group.

Administrative Structure: Staffing and Supervision

Family Preservation Services is staffed by a full-time director and a full-time associate director, both of whom carry family preservation cases. Both hold advanced degrees in psychology. The staff also comprises other full-time practitioners and several part-time consultants employed as practitioners on a fee-for-service basis. Staff members receive at least one hour a week of clinical supervision with the director, and one and one-half hours a week of clinical group supervision.

Program Design: Initial Phases

Referrals.   Referrals come from the Department of Social Services (DSS) and the courts. Staff members meet with the referring workers and the family for the first interview. When appropriate, parents are often encouraged to call Beacon Counseling themselves.

Case selection.   The following are the criteria for acceptance to the Parent Partner Program:

> A family in which a child or children under the age of 16 will be removed from the home within 48 hours
>
> A family from which a child or children have been removed temporarily within the two weeks before referral
>
> A family with parents who want the children to remain in or return to live with the family
>
> A situation where there is no threat to the physical safety of the staff and family members

The families who are served come from the poorer African-American, Caribbean, Latino, and Caucasian neighborhoods of Boston, and present a range of family problems, such as child abuse and neglect; lack of housing, medical care, and adequate food; juvenile delinquency; and parent-child conflicts.

Intake/assessment.   Within 48 hours of a referral, the director or associate director makes arrangements to meet the referring workers and the family in the family's home or in the court or in other community sites. A review of the reasons for the referral and the goals of the referral source takes place. Staff members interview parents alone to assess their willingness and capacity to participate in the program, and also with the DSS worker and the parents to assess their understanding of what is required of them, their willingness to cooperate, and the risk of physical danger to the staff. A decision is made immediately as to whether to take the case, request support services from DSS, and begin crisis intervention services with the family. If a case is accepted, DSS retains legal responsibility for the welfare and protection of the children.

Program Design: Service Delivery

Duration. The agency works with families 30 days, providing intensive, crisis intervention, and parent support services. Families may then participate in weekly two-hour therapy sessions and/or a parent group, as needed.

Intensity. The intensity of service depends upon the needs of the family. Families may be assigned a Family Practitioner and a paraprofessional Parent Partner Family Practitioner. Caseloads range from four to ten families at a time. Parent Partners are involved with only two or three cases at a time. The Parent Partner may spend 20 to 25 hours in the home during the first seven days, if necessary to assure the safety of the children.

Visits are generally open-ended during the crisis intervention phase of service and are then two hours weekly when the crisis is resolved and the family requests continuing involvement. Families can choose individual, couple, family, or group therapy.

Staff members are accessible for on-call support as needed through the use of beepers and a seven-day, 24-hour answering service.

Site. Family preservation services take place primarily in the family's home. Support groups and some therapy sessions may take place in the Beacon Counseling offices.

Services. The program provides emergency, intensive services to families who are in a crisis that might lead to the placement of one or more children outside the family, with the goal of empowering parents to care for their children. Services are based on a family systems model of family therapy, emphasizing changed behavior through structural/strategic therapy, providing significant information, and emergency concrete services. To elaborate: the program offers outreach mental health services with a focus on action and change in behavior. The emphasis is on structuring shifts in family relationships that promote changes in patterns of interaction among family members; the staff seeks to strengthen and empower parents and to assess the family's needs for supplemental services.

Funding

Beacon Counseling bills Medicaid for eligible families, and also receives funding from the Boston Juvenile Court and private donations. The Edna McConnell Clark Foundation provided initial funding in 1985 for the family preservation services.

Behavioral Sciences Institute
HOMEBUILDERS DIVISION
1717 S. 341ST PLACE
FEDERAL WAY, WASHINGTON 98003
(206) 874-3630

Program History and Background

Behavioral Sciences Institute is a voluntary, not-for-profit agency formed in 1981 to provide Homebuilders family preservation services and to study and disseminate information regarding in-home services as an alternative to out-of-home placement. The Homebuilders program began in 1974, in Tacoma, Washington and was affiliated with Catholic Community Services until 1981.

Homebuilders is an intensive, in-home crisis intervention and family education program. It was designed to work with the most seriously troubled families in the state of Washington. The goal of the program is to prevent the need for out-of-home placement of family members through the provision of immediate, in-home crisis intervention and skills-based treatment. Services are aimed at diffusing the crisis and teaching families new skills to preclude crisis recurrence and to help the members live together as a family.

Behavioral Sciences has direct service, research, and training divisions, and offers consultation and extensive training for a fee to public and private agencies.

Administrative Structure: Staffing, Supervision, Training

Behavioral Sciences Institute is administered by two codirectors, both with Ph.D. degrees in psychology. There are also an associate director with a master's degree in social work, a director of training with a Ph.D. in psychology, and an assistant director with a master's degree in social work.

Homebuilders in Washington has an intake coordinator, intake workers in the satellite offices, six part-time supervisors, and 24 full-time practitioners. New practitioners participate in eight or nine days of intensive, skills-based workshop training and all staff members have the opportunity to participate in in-service and outside training.

Practitioners and supervisors have master's degrees in psychology, social work, or related fields. Full-time practitioners work with two families at a time; part-time supervisors work with one family in addition to supervising four workers each. Staff members operate out of three offices that serve four counties throughout Washington. New staff candidates are interviewed extensively and asked to participate in role-play simulations of family sessions to permit assessment of their skills with families and their interactions with the staff. Supervisors carry the first few cases with new practitioners to provide intensive supervision and training. Ongoing individual and weekly group supervision is routinely provided for all staff members. Practitioners are strongly and sensitively supported by supervisors and administrators to keep burnout or overload to a minimum.

Program Design: Initial Phases

Referrals.   Referrals come from the Department of Social Services/ Child Protective Services (abuse and neglect) and Family Reconciliation Services (parent-child conflicts). Homebuilders is contacted when other services have not helped the family to resolve problems leading to the current crisis, and one or more children are in imminent danger of being placed out of the home.

Case selection.   Families are viewed as appropriate referrals if, without the agency's services, one or more children would be placed outside the home. The referral source must be able to document that placement would indeed take place.

The Homebuilders philosophy is that no family is considered hopeless, and that all families are potentially workable. Therefore all families referred are considered for acceptance, unless (1) there is no room in the program; (2) the family situation could be better handled by a less intensive service; (3) the family situation is assessed as too dangerous for family members and staff members; or (4) the family refuses service.

Families seen by Homebuilders include single parents and those with two parents present in the home. Families fall within several stages of the family life cycle, including adolescent parents; young parents with young children; and parents with adolescent children. Some parents work, and many receive public assistance. The majority of families are white; a small percentage are black, Asian, Hispanic, or Native American. Most families are described as experiencing a sense of social isolation, whether living in rural or urban areas.

Family problems vary, and have included runaways, juvenile delinquents, parent-child conflicts, parents or children with severe depression, suicidal thoughts, alcohol or drug addiction, autism, mental retardation, and psychosis. Child sexual abuse, physical abuse, and serious neglect are also problems Homebuilders has addressed. In addition, problems have included children with school-related difficulties, family violence, medical illnesses, unemployment, and families with situational or chronic problems.

Intake/assessment. Upon referral, appropriate cases are screened by an intake worker and assigned to an available practitioner. The referral source is asked to discuss the Homebuilders alternative with the family before the referral is made. The Homebuilders practitioner then contacts the family the same day and is available to arrange for a visit within 24 hours in the family's home.

Initial family assessments begin with the first intake session and continue during the first few visits with the family. Homebuilders emphasizes an "active listening" (reflective listening) approach to gathering information and developing an initial rapport with families. This approach allows family members to describe their situation with a minimum of intervening questions from the practitioners. Family members are therefore able to talk freely, allowing their perceptions of their strengths and problems to evolve gradually, and practitioners are able to create a supportive, nonjudgmental atmosphere. Families are encouraged to identify their problems and needs and to make decisions about how the initial phases of work will begin. Practitioners and family members together identify areas for work, and specify two to four major goals and other tasks that can be achieved within one month's time. The focus of involvement is on diffusing the crisis and the associated emotions engaging the family members, and identifying ways that the situation can be changed.

Program Design: Service Delivery

Duration/intensity. Homebuilders practitioners work with families for a period of four weeks. If necessary, extensions of up to two weeks can be added. Practitioners carry two families at a time and work with them as often as is needed within the one month period. The average amount of time spent with a family varies from eight to ten hours a week, depending upon the needs of the family. Practitioners are on call 24 hours a day, seven days a week. Supervisors serve as back-up in the event of a crisis. Families are encouraged to call practitioners when they feel pressed to report progress, or for monitoring progress, and are given the office number, the practitioners' home telephone numbers and the supervisors' home telephone numbers. A back-up beeper system is used when the families cannot reach the staff directly. One person from each county carries the beeper for one week at a time.

Homebuilders selected the four-week service period from its experience and from information from research about crisis intervention, which has shown that when people are in crisis, they are believed to be most open to change. A crisis typically lasts from four to six weeks, and it is during this period that families have been found to be most responsive to outside intervention and support. Therefore, crisis intervention services are brief and intensive to maximize the use of the state of crisis. Homebuilders had also found that by providing intensive, open-ended educational interventions and supports to families when they are in crisis, families are responsive and able to quickly learn new skills for managing their problems. The key is having time-limited and goal-oriented services available *during* the crisis period.

Site.   Homebuilders services take place in the family's home or natural community environment (e.g., school, playground), not in agency offices.

Services.   Homebuilders practitioners provide a mix of therapeutic, educational, and supportive services to teach family members new skills. These skills can then be called upon the next time there is a crisis situation, or can be used to prevent similar crises from occurring. Practitioners also provide concrete services such as transportation and locating food and clothing to help families meet basic needs.

Behavioral strategies, rational emotive therapy, training (e.g., communication, assertiveness, problem-solving, cognitive, anger management) and structuring strategies such as crisis cards and goal attainment scaling are approaches used to help family members learn to make necessary changes and to monitor their progress. Goal attainment scaling identifies the minimum acceptable goal and breaks it down into manageable pieces. This method of measuring progress toward meeting goals helps family members and the practitioners stay focused, see progress, and identify where greater effort is needed.

Homebuilders practitioners spend time in the family's home teaching and modeling effective child management skills and teaching parents new ways of setting consistent limits, using positive methods of discipline, communication, and solving problems.

Advocacy and networking with other social services agencies and with informal supports are important parts of the Homebuilders program, as is advocacy for state and national social change.

Evaluation and Success Rates

Homebuilders conducts extensive evaluations of services provided, populations served, and effectiveness of service delivery. At three months after case closure an average of 94% of the families served from 1974-85 have remained intact. Eighty-eight percent of the families reviewed since 1983 at one year after case closure have remained together.

Funding

Homebuilders crisis intervention services are funded by the state of Washington. In the spring of 1987, Behavioral Sciences Institute was funded by the Edna McConnell Foundation to begin a Homebuilders program in the Bronx, New York.

Centers for New Horizons
FAMILY DEVELOPMENT INSTITUTE
3950 SOUTH STATE STREET
CHICAGO, ILLINOIS 60609
(312) 624-7630

History and Background

Centers For New Horizons was established in 1971 as an independent not-for-profit community organization for the purpose of administering five early childhood centers and a community development program on Chicago's South Side. Over the years the organization has expanded to include an elementary school, after-school programs, a tutorial program, a day school for emotionally disturbed adolescents, and three counseling programs, one of which is the Family Development Institute. The other two include an in-home counseling program for families referred by the Department of Children and Family Services for abuse and neglect problems, and a program for families with developmentally delayed or handicapped young children.

The Family Development Institute (FDI) was formed in the summer of 1984 and serves families whose children are at risk of placement, or those with children already placed outside the home. FDI provides a structured classroom-educational approach to helping parents learn parenting, home management, and personal development skills. Classes take place in the program's offices on the upper floor of a community center-day care center within one of the South Side's high-rise public housing developments. Since January 1986, when the current director took over the program, FDI has included in-home counseling.

Administrative Structure: Staffing, Supervision, Training

The director of counseling administers the agency's three counseling programs. Other staff members include a full-time administrative coordinator, crisis workers, and a job developer for clients. The program uses outside consultants as teachers for G.E.D., parenting, stress management, nutrition, office skills, and fitness classes. These teachers come from local colleges or other community positions and work part-time in the program. All professional staff members are supervised by the director of counseling. Staff members have received training in G.I.F.T.—Gestalt Integrating Family Therapy—which includes a family systems orientation, and have attended biweekly training sessions in family therapy techniques.

Program Design: Initial Phases

Referrals. Referrals come from other programs of the agency and word of mouth from past program participants.

Case selection. Families are accepted into the program if they are in the following groups:

Second generation welfare recipients

Living in a public housing development

Have had a child during their adolescent years

The young single black parents with young children have been described by the staff as having low self-esteem, and as being under-developed, with untapped potential; they are unaware of their own power and abilities. Family problems include abuse and neglect; poor nutrition, medical care, and housing; depression, lethargy and lack of energy; family violence; poor parenting skills; drug and alcohol dependency; and relationship problems.

Intake/assessment.   Within a few days of the referral, the family is interviewed and evaluated by a member of the staff and then evaluated by the team (director and staff) for appropriateness for the program. Information about the family's social history is gathered, including medical and nutritional, stress management, parenting abilities, and educational/vocational skills. Individual goals are established. Activities include participation in classroom experiences as well as individual counseling with a staff member.

Program Design: Service Delivery

Duration/intensity.   The Family Development Institute has experimented with different time periods for the classroom component of the program. Presently each cohort of classes runs for 15 weeks, with 20 parents participating. Classes meet three days a week from nine to three; a well-balanced lunch is included. On the other two days parents meet with staff members for support counseling and home visits. Parents spend an average of 18 to 20 hours a week with the staff in classes and individually.

Staff members carry caseloads of seven or eight families active in the classroom phase, and 20 to 30 families for follow-up support and job placement.

Site.   Classes take place at the program's office. The building also houses a recreational after-school program and a day care center for participants' children. Counseling takes place in the office or in the families' homes.

Services.   The program supports the parents' individual emotional, intellectual, social, and physical development, and promotes self-sufficiency by offering classes to improve their vocational skills, with a job developer's help in finding job placements. Classes also include nutrition; stress management; G.E.D. preparation (math, reading, language); office skills; parent education; physical fitness (exercise); sewing and cooking; and family planning. Participants are paid five dollars a day for attending the program.

The theme of powerlessness is dealt with throughout the program. Participants are encouraged to accept and understand their own responsibility in what happens to them. They are taught new problem-solving skills as well as supported in dealing with painful feelings about their past experiences. Parents are taught how to meet their own needs, how to find and use outside resources, and how to more effectively meet the needs of their children. Casework counseling is offered to support changes parents make in classes. Staff members provide role models and teach parents more effective home management skills during home visits.

At the end of the 15-week classroom phase, family cases are not closed. Staff members work with families until goals are met, often for as long as a year after the classroom phase ends.

Evaluation and Success Rates

Between August 1985 and August 1986, FDI served 62 families— 22 with children living at home and 40 whose children were in foster care. All of the families with children at home remained intact, and all of the families with children in placement were able to have their children return home at the end of the classroom phase of services. For 50 families served between January 1987 and July 1988, all of the children were living at home at case closing.

Funding

The agency estimates that it costs $2,580 per family for the 15-week classroom phase. The Edna McConnell Clark Foundation funded the program for two years. The program receives funding from the State Department of Children and Family Services, the United Way, and private foundations.

Commonweal Family Consulting Services
FAMILY PRESERVATION PROGRAM
3 HARBOR DRIVE, SUITE 111
SAUSALITO, CALIFORNIA 94965
(415) 331-6033

History and Background

For the past decade Commonweal Family Consulting Services (Commonweal), in affiliation with the Growing Mind Corporation, has provided a network of schools and diagnostic assessment services to at-risk youths and their families. Commonweal has been among the pioneers in the psychology and medical fields in studying the relationships between food sensitivities and children's behavioral problems.

In June 1984 Commonweal began to provide emergency in-home services and diagnostic assessments to families at risk of having a child placed outside the home. The project serves Marin, Alameda, Contra Costa, and San Francisco Counties. It is Commonweal's philosophy that family dissolution can sometimes be avoided if adequate diagnostic information about family's problems can be offered at a critical point during a family crisis. Commonweal was formed to provide parents and children with access to diagnostic assessments related to the family's particular problems. The varied psychological and medical assessments make it possible for families to have accurate information about children's difficulties and provide the basis for future planning for the family's health, educational, or psychological needs.

Administrative Structure: Staffing, Caseloads, Supervision, Training

Commonweal employs a team of three experienced staff members. The director, a psychologist, is responsible for fund-raising, maintaining relationships with referral sources and consultants, intake, and a caseload of two families. The assistant director screens and conducts intake, carries two cases, and monitors administrative aspects of the program. A half-time clinical social work supervisor carries one case, and supervises all intakes and all counselors who are training at Commonweal. Staff members carry from two to four families for follow-up contacts. The program serves five families intensively for two months. It has a capacity of 50 families a year.

In addition to the three salaried staff members, Commonweal uses a large network of consulting professionals to provide the individualized diagnostic assessments of children and parents. These consultants provide the agency's core services and are professionals in the fields of pediatrics, nutrition, child psychiatry, clinical psychology, speech and language pathology, and learning disabilities evaluation. The agency also uses a group home counselor who provides temporary respite services to children who require brief time-out periods, and who can return to their families within a week or two.

Commonweal periodically holds training days for all staff members and other involved professionals to review cases, evaluate progress, and share new developments in the medical and psychological fields.

An advisory board with members from each of the four counties served, representing the judicial, medical, educational, and political systems on both local and national levels, meets annually.

Program Design: Initial Phases

Referrals.   Referral sources include a variety of public and private agencies or concerned citizens, including the courts, county departments of social services, health professionals, teachers, relatives, and concerned friends or family members. Referrals may also come from community counseling agencies or overnight shelters.

Case selection.   Referrals are initially screened by the staff to confirm the need for placement were Commonweal not available. A family is considered appropriate if there is a child under 18 at risk of placement, if the family situation is safe for family members and the staff, and if the family agrees to work intensively with the Commonweal staff and consultants.

Approximately 24% of the families served during the first year were black, 10% Hispanic, and 66% white. Two-thirds of the referrals came from Alameda and Marin Counties, with one-third from San Francisco and Contra Costa Counties. The families served tend to have older children, typically junior and senior high school age, whose parents are described as "feeling out of control." Adolescents have often had a history of involvement with the juvenile justice system.

The families are primarily middle-class families who have difficulty solving problems and communicating with each other. Other family problems include chronic truancy, runaway or out-of-control behavior, sexual or physical abuse, emotional neglect, substance abuse, juvenile delinquency, serious parent-child conflicts, and marital discord.

Intake/assessment.   When the agency receives a referral, information is gathered by the director or assistant director about the family's problems and history. The family is immediately contacted to arrange for an intake interview, which takes place in the family's home or at other community sites. Two staff members meet with the family for two to three hours to explain the program's services, develop a case history, establish family goals, and determine the need for further professional evaluations. Initial interviews are held with family members together and separately to add to the staff's understanding of the family's situation.

The initial family assessment is conducted within the framework of the following considerations:

> Biochemical problems
> Family dynamics and communication patterns
> School performance problems
> Learning problems
> Medical problems
> Speech and language difficulties
> Psychiatric or neurological problems
> Nutritional deficiencies

A case plan is developed within 48 hours of the referral, based upon information collected from the referral source and during the initial interviews with the family. This plan may include referrals to appropriate consultants and family therapy provided by Commonweal. If the family is already involved with other counselors, the agency coordinates its services with them.

Program Design: Service Delivery

Duration.   Staff members work with families for a period of two months, or sometimes longer if there are delays in arranging for appointments with consultants. A follow-up period may last three to four months longer to allow for contacts with schools and other agencies to be sure services are in place, and to be available for further support to families. Follow-up contact typically takes place over the telephone.

Intensity. Staff members spend approximately 36 hours with families during the two-month period, with an average of 20 hours during the first two weeks of assessment and service coordination. During the diagnostic period, less intensive time is spent in supportive counseling with families. During the final week or two, a more concentrated period of time is spent summarizing reports and arranging for follow-up services. Staff members are available 24 hours a day by telephone or an emergency beeper number.

Site. Services are delivered in the family's home and community. This enables the staff to observe the child and family's interactions in the natural environment. Staff members may also accompany family members to other agencies for appointments.

Services. Each case requires a different mix of diagnostic assessments and services tailored to the needs of each family member. After a careful evaluation of all intake data, a case plan is developed and appropriate diagnostic referrals are made to consultants in the community. The case plan may include one or more of the following services and evaluations:

Physical, neurological, nutritional, or allergy examination by a physician

Thorough blood chemistry evaluation and/or glucose tolerance tests

Toxic metal screening with mineral analyses

Speech and language evaluations

Complete psychological assessments with a focus on the child's ability to learn

Follow-up visits with physician, speech and language pathologist, and/or clinical psychologist as necessary

Two months of intensive family therapy and training in parenting skills

Referral to an educational advocate to represent the client at the school district level

The biochemical evaluations determine whether certain chemical imbalances are affecting a child's out-of-control behavior. Psychological and neurological evaluations analyze the child's ability to learn, to process information and remember what was read. A nutritional analysis evaluates the effects of food allergies on the child's overall mood and behaviors.

Over the two-month period of intensive services, activity with the family might include visits to the family's home to help resolve sudden or ongoing conflicts and teach new communication skills; training in parenting skills; visits to courts or probation offices; conferences with teachers or other school personnel; help in obtaining a job or arranging for job training; and direct referrals and advocacy concerning food/housing/social services needs. When the agency finds that in-home services are not able to keep the family together, staff members typically remain involved in planning for an appropriate setting for the child and in following up on the child's progress while in placement.

The completion of all diagnostic work and the development of recommendations for future services take two months. During this time families and staff members meet with consultants two to three times. The staff then prepares for the family members a final summary of the diagnostic evaluations, with recommendations for additional services, or changes in diet, or family communication patterns. With the family's permission, the staff shares the report with referral sources, schools, and courts.

The purpose of gathering such detailed information about each family is to "reframe" for the family the current problems. Reframing refers to the way the new diagnostic information about medical conditions or behavioral difficulties can be used to take self-blame away from children and parents for the troubles they are experiencing. New reasons for old problems are discovered; the situation is then reframed in terms of the relationships between learning problems and social skills impairment; biochemical imbalances and emotional problems; or nutritional deficiencies and behavioral mood swings. With new information about these behavior problems, family members feel relief in knowing that the child is not intentionally "bad"; rather, there are concrete causes for the distress. The staff can then teach parents how to change communication patterns and/or diets to meet the special needs of a child. The end of the agency's services often serves as the beginning for future planning.

Evaluation and Success Rates

From October 1984 to November 1985, 51 families were served. At case closing 80% of the children remained in parental custody; 12%

were in alternative placements upon the referral of Commonweal or other agency; 6% had been placed without completing the services provided by Commonweal; and one child (2%) became an emancipated minor and did not complete the program.

Funding

Commonweal has had a two-year Edna McConnell Clark Foundation grant to cover the salaries of the director, assistant director, and the clinical social worker. Consultants are paid by a three-year grant from the Office of Criminal Justice Planning, as are counselors trained by Commonweal. Private insurance and Medicaid reimbursements also cover some diagnostic evaluations with the psychologist and pediatrician. A fee-for-service training program on the Commonweal method of family assessment using community consultants is being developed, to be offered to public and voluntary agency workers.

Home Education Livelihood Program
3423 CENTRAL AVENUE, NE
ALBUQUERQUE, NEW MEXICO 87106
(505) 265-3717

History and Background

The Home Education Livelihood Program (HELP) is a nonprofit community development corporation operating in economically depressed areas throughout the state of New Mexico. Incorporated since 1965, it has served approximately 125,000 farmworkers, their families, and other low-income groups who subsist far below the poverty level. In its diversified social and economic projects it directly reaches low-income Spanish-Americans (in Northern New Mexico), Mexican-Americans, and Native-Americans (Navajo and Pueblo) through its many centers and projects in rural and urban communities.

The name of the agency, Home Education Livelihood Program, reflects the basic philosophy and mission statement of the agency—to provide comprehensive services to the total family as a means of enhancing the family's well-being. As such, HELP provides a variety of supportive services to individuals and families: housing, child development, emergency assistance, nutrition education, and job training. Since 1986 the agency has offered family preservation services.

Administrative Structure: Staffing, Supervision, and Training

The family preservation program has four full-time staff members: a coordinator, two family practitioners, and a secretary. The coordinator spends half-time in project management and half-time carrying cases. Practitioners carry two cases at a time. The family preservation program presently can serve up to 50 families a year.

Intake/Assessment

Referrals. Referrals come from the CHINS Department of Juvenile Probation and from the Human Services Department (HSD), which must indicate that without family preservation intervention, out-of-home placement of the children is the most likely course of treatment. Referral workers provide information by phone to the coordinator or a practitioner who screens the case according to HELP criteria. If a family is eligible, a visit with the family is scheduled to take place within 48 hours. During this first home visit, an initial assessment is made of the family's willingness to work with the program and the appropriateness of a short-term intensive service for the family's needs. After this visit, a decision is made as to whether the case will be accepted, and the referring worker is notified by phone.

Case selection. The referral source and family members must be in agreement that unless intensive treatment occurs, out-of-home placement in a foster home, a group home, or a psychiatric facility is imminent for at least one family member age 17 or younger. (The HSD staff must be able to document that placement will eventuate without family preservation services.) All must agree that all other less intensive community services have been exhausted or will not suffice, and that their goal is to have the child(ren) remain in or return to the home of the legal guardian. The parent or legal guardian must be willing to sign an authorization-for-treatment form. If the child is currently out of the home, there must be a plan and an agreement for the child's return home within seven days of family preservation intake.

Cases are ineligible if one or more of the following situations exist:

All family members refuse services or the legal guardian refuses to sign an authorization-for-treatment form.

The referral source, the family preservation staff, and the family members agree that placement is not imminent or that less intensive services would suffice.

There is no plan and/or agreement for the child(ren) to return home within seven days of intake.

The parent has made other out-of-home living arrangements for the child(ren).

Placement would be with a noncustodial relative or friend, and there is no goal of returning the child(ren) to the parent's home.

The only goal of the referring worker is to have family preservation service assess the family to determine if placement is appropriate.

Program Design

Duration.   Practitioners initially provide crisis intervention with families, followed by intensive home-based counseling, for four to six weeks.

Intensity.   Families receive an average of eight to ten hours of therapy a week. In addition, up to four hours a week of collateral work is spent with community agencies accessing services needed by the clients, totaling at least 56 hours of service a month.

Site.   Practitioners see families in their own homes, where the problems are occurring.

Services.   Besides home-based family therapy, the family preservation program provides hard services such as assisting client families in obtaining food, clothing, shelter, housing, employment, legal aid, and medical attention. The program also advocates for client families with the schools and the courts, and collaborates with other community mental health services to provide a continuity of care for client families. These actions empower families to gain access to services and reduce dependency.

HELP also offers a range of services through contracts with HSD as part of the Community Services Block Grant and the Migrant/Season Farmworker Community Services Block Grant. These services are made available to eligible family preservation clients.

The family preservation program uses goal attainment scaling to measure progress toward family goals for intervention. Goals are recalibrated weekly. Family members usually identify one to three goals for intervention, for example, increasing the parents' child management skills, increasing their anger management skills, and alleviating the family's financial stress.

Evaluation and Success Rate

A follow-up evaluation of client families found that 80% remained intact three months after the case was closed.

Funding

HELP received a two-year grant from the Edna McConnell Clark Foundation to develop its family preservation program. Funding was subsequently picked up by the Human Services Department.

Kingsley House
FAMILY PRESERVATION SERVICES
914 RICHARD STREET
NEW ORLEANS, LOUISIANA 70130
(504) 523-6221

History and Background

Kingsley House, begun in 1896, is the oldest settlement house in the South. It is adjacent to a housing project and offers programs for preschool and school-age children and for adolescents, as well as parents and senior citizens.

The Family Preservation Services Project began serving families in October 1985. It is an intensive home-based, crisis intervention program providing an array of services to families who are at risk of immediate breakup, to help families acquire improved coping skills and to create change in the family's situation that will enable the family to remain together safely.

Administrative Structure: Staffing, Supervision, Training

The project is administered by a full-time M.S.W. program manager, who supervises master's-level social workers, a screener, and a secretary. Two hours a week are spent in staff development/supervision, including a focus on case reviews and new therapeutic approaches.

Program Design: Initial Phases

Referrals.   Referrals come from the Family Services Unit of the Office of Community Services (OCS), the New Orleans public child welfare agency. Family preservation services staff members have worked closely with OCS to identify families at risk of immediate dissolution. Referrals may also go through OCS from the New Orleans Police Department's Child Abuse Unit. Specially assigned and trained plainclothes police officers investigate child abuse and neglect reports jointly with OCS workers. Referrals also are received from the Office of Mental Health and the Juvenile Court.

Case selection.   The project serves families as an alternative to foster care placement, and therefore provides help to high-risk multi-problem families when all other services have been tried, and serious problems persist that could lead to the placement of one or more children outside the family.

The families have experienced chronic and situational abuse and neglect, runaway adolescents, medical neglect, and severe parent-child conflicts. Families involved in sexual abuse are not accepted because of the length of time needed to work with such problems. Active psychosis of a family member is another problem that the program does not accept for service. Families served since the program started have been multiproblem poor families, both black and white. Families have had younger and older children and have required therapeutic, educational, and concrete services.

Intake/assessment.   Referral sources call the screener, who takes the referral information. A worker is assigned and makes a home visit within 24 hours to assess the family's situation, and to determine whether the family would be appropriate for the program.

Program Design: Service Delivery

Duration/intensity.   Intensive, in-home family services are provided for a six-week period. Social work staff members carry two to three families for this period. An additional three-month period of less intensive follow-up and support services is also provided to each family. Staff members carry three to four follow-up cases at a time. The referring agency retains case planning responsibility throughout.

During the follow-up phase, the program staff members serve as advocates and liaisons to other community services, as needed. On the average, a staff member spends at least ten hours a week with a family during the six-week intensive services phase. Staff members are on-call 24 hours a day, seven days a week, and give families their home phone numbers. So far, the families have not used these numbers excessively.

Site. Services take place in families' homes. Occasionally families may be seen in the Kingsley House offices when family members attend other agency programs, such as the parent-child center.

Services. The program works with families who are experiencing the most serious problems involving abuse, neglect, poverty, environmental stresses, and parent-child conflicts. An eclectic social casework and family systems approach is used to teach family members new problem-solving and coping skills. Parents are taught how to manage their children's behavior and how to more effectively meet their children's developmental needs.

A combination of family counseling, supportive casework, and concrete services is offered to families in crisis. Much work is done on environmental stresses, helping families to fix up existing housing or to find other more suitable housing. Limited emergency cash and goods are available through the original grants. One or two referrals have involved intensive reunification services for families whose children are to return home imminently.

Evaluation and Success Rates

From October 1985 through February 1989 the program worked with 82 families, including 298 children. Placements were experienced by three families involving four children.

Funding

The project was originally funded through a grant from the Edna McConnell Clark Foundation. It is now funded through contracts with the Office of Community Services and the Office of Mental Health.

Family Preservation Project

CHILD AND FAMILY SERVICES
VANCE, GRANVILLE, WARREN, FRANKLIN AREA MENTAL HEALTH
DEPARTMENT OF MENTAL HEALTH/MENTAL RETARDATION/
SUBSTANCE ABUSE
125 EMERGENCY ROAD
HENDERSON, NORTH CAROLINA 27536
(919) 492-9191

History and Background

In 1984 the Child and Family Services program of the North Carolina Division of Mental Health received a grant from the Edna McConnell Clark Foundation, along with public mental health funds, to establish the Family Preservation Project. The project provides intensive, home-based emergency services to prevent the unnecessary separation of children from their families. A four-county area in north central North Carolina (Vance, Granville, Warren and Franklin counties) was selected for the site. The area's Mental Health Division had already demonstrated a strong commitment to preserving families through its effective work with very difficult family situations. A strong joint programming effort also existed in this four-county area across the three major child serving agencies: mental health, social services and juvenile court. These relationships were considered to be a critical foundation for the success of the project.

The four counties of the north central region represent much of North Carolina, with a sparse total population of 117,000, one-half of whom are minority and almost one-fourth of whom have incomes below the poverty level.

Child and Family Services, the public mental health program, has three units: Day Treatment, Out-Patient, and Residential Care Services. The project is part of the Residential Care Unit because of its already existing continuum of in-home services to prevent placements or promote reunification of families.

Administrative Structure: Staffing, Caseloads, Supervision, Training

The project has two full-time home-based practitioners, who each carry two families, and one half-time home-based practitioner. Five families can be served at a time for an eight-week cycle, with a capacity of 30 families a year.

The staff members are included in the ongoing training provided by the Area Mental Health Division. The home-based practitioners receive administrative supervision from the project coordinator, and weekly clinical supervision from the director of outpatient services. This arrangement accommodates pre-program supervisory relationships.

The staff meets weekly in a study group with the director of Child and Family Services and the community residential care staff to review cases, provide support, and reduce the sense of isolation in doing outreach work. To avoid burnout, staff members have the option of periodically taking a short break between cases, usually no longer than four to five days.

In an emergency, staff members are available to clients by telephone 24 hours a day, seven days a week. On weekends and evenings, families may reach the staff by calling the Mental Health Department's After-Hours Emergency Services, whose staff contacts the project staff. Backup coverage for the project staff includes the director of Child and Family Services as well as the residential care staff.

Program Design: Initial Phases

Referrals. Referrals come from agencies in all four counties: the Juvenile Court Probation Services; the Department of Social Services (DSS)/Child Protective Units; and the Mental Health Division.

Case selection. Representatives of the project, DSS, and the Juvenile Court Probation Services meet whenever an opening exists in the project to discuss potential referrals and the selection of the family most in need of family preservation services. Families are selected for the project if the referral source and the project staff determine that a crisis exists and that the family situation is serious enough to require forced removal of a child from the family. Several other criteria are considered in the case selection process, including the safety of family and staff members; whether less intensive services have been tried or would be feasible; the number of children at risk in the family; and the age of the children at risk. Acceptance into the program also depends upon the family's willingness to participate in the services.

Imminence of placement is narrowly defined. Families are considered for acceptance only at the point when placement would take place within a day or two or when there is an adjourned court date at which time placement would be ordered. The project is viewed as the last "reasonable effort" tried before a child is removed.

Families served by the project are described by the staff as multiproblem families, with a wide range of social and emotional difficulties. Problems include serious emotional/mental illness; violent/aggressive antisocial behaviors (involving guns and other weapons); child abuse/neglect; suspected sexual abuse; juvenile delinquency; runaway children; and substance abuse.

Intake/assessment. The case selection process involves family assessment by the referral sources and the project staff. Both DSS and the Court Probation Services report examining family problems and treatment alternatives more creatively as a result of the referral and case selection process for the project.

Home visits are made at the family's convenience within 24 hours of the referral. Initial family assessments by the project staff consider what the referral source defined as the presenting problem, and how the family members perceive their problems. Staff members explain the brief duration of the intervention to the family, and together they establish goals to be accomplished within the short time frame. Assessment with the family of its situation and progress is ongoing. Weekly staff meetings are also held to review each family's problems, and progress made toward the goals set. New areas for work are assessed, resources are identified, and strategies are developed for working with the families and advocating with other agencies.

Program Design: Service Delivery

Duration. Services are offered to families for a maximum of eight weeks. Staff members believe that time-limited service creates a pressure period in which to accomplish identified goals, while reducing family dependency on workers.

The project has the capacity to provide "booster shots" to families previously served, including crisis telephone contacts or in-person visits if needed. Families may also participate in a second eight-week cycle if the risk of removal exists again.

Intensity.   High intensity and frequency of service are available up to 20 hours per week, an average of 12 hours a week spent with families. Visits are arranged whenever possible to accommodate the schedule of the family members, including an extensive use of evening hours. The length of visits may vary, and depends upon the family's situation on a particular day. Typically the most intensive work takes place during the initial four weeks, with the final weeks used to phase down services from a crisis level to one of ongoing support, or to consolidate a needed network of connections with other community programs.

Site.   Services are delivered primarily in the family's home or community. Staff members describe the clients as families who have difficulty making and keeping mental health and social service appointments. Outreach to clients' homes has proven effective in engaging these types of families, both in the project and in other mental health programs in this region of North Carolina.

Services.   A variety of services are available through the project and its linkages with other community resources, with the goals of keeping the families together and stabilized. Services include intensive family and individual counseling; parenting, communication, negotiation, and behavior management skills; and the teaching of techniques related to housekeeping, nutrition, and budgeting. The workers are particularly skilled at diffusing potentially violent situations.

The project's solid relationships with other community services and with its referral sources are critical components. The project staff seeks in the long run to establish a network of appropriate services for families and children. It is this advocacy with other programs that provides families with the supports necessary to maintain gains once the project has ended. Other programs may include day treatment services; less intensive in-home counseling and support services; recreational activities (summer and after-school); day care; and outpatient mental health services.

Services are delivered within the context of family systems and structural family therapy theories. Staff members include family members in setting limited yet realistic goals appropriate for brief intervention, and directed toward stabilizing the present crisis and obtaining needed services for the present and future. Helping families learn how to advocate for themselves is emphasized. No single intervention model is used; rather, services and strategies are planned to meet the individual needs of family members.

Evaluation and Success Rates

From March 1985, when the project accepted its first families, to June 1989, 85 families that included 196 children were served. Three months after termination, 75% of the families polled had remained intact. Staff members from the North Carolina Mental Health Training Division are responsible for conducting the three-month follow-up contacts with families. Families have also routinely kept in touch with project staff members after case closure, primarily for booster shot support.

Funding

The project was initially funded by a grant from the Edna McConnell Clark Foundation and by funds from the state Department of Mental Health. Subsequently, the project continued with the support of state mental health funds.

Sweetser Children's Home
FAMILY PRESERVATION SERVICES PROGRAM
50 MOODY STREET
SACO, MAINE 04072
(207) 284-5981

History and Background

Sweetser Children's Home, founded in 1828, is the oldest residential treatment center in Maine. Over the years, Sweetser has grown to its present array of residential, group home, educational, and community psychiatric services for emotionally disturbed children and their families.

In October 1984 Sweetser received a grant from the Edna McConnell Clark Foundation to provide in-home, intensive family therapy and social services to families to prevent the need for placement of children outside their homes. The Sweetser Family Preservation Program joined an already existing network of short-term, home-based, intensive services within the state of Maine—programs funded by four separate human service departments: education, social services, mental health, and juvenile justice.

The Family Preservation Program serves families from York County in southern Maine. Over the past ten years, York County has become Maine's fastest growing and most densely populated area, with an increase in single-parent families and the associated stresses and problems. The population of the county is predominantly white and working class, with 10% living at the poverty level.

Administrative Structure: Staffing, Caseloads, Supervision, Training

Four staff members work in teams of two, consisting of an M.S.W. and a bachelor's-level practitioner. Teams are supervised by a half-time M.S.W. treatment supervisor, who also supervises two bachelor's- or master's-level social work students. The program is administered one-fourth time by the director of community services.

Each team works with four families at a time, with a service capacity of 48 families a year, including student cases. Teams allow for shared responsibilities and provide workers with support and feedback. Staff members have found that working in teams often offers safety in potentially violent situations. Team members have differentiated responsibilities, and alternate the role of lead person. B.S.W. practitioners often lead when cases require primarily concrete or basic-needs services; M.S.W. practitioners assume the leadership role when interpersonal family relationships are the main problem. M.S.W. practitioners are described as having higher levels of clinical skills and more experience in working with difficult families.

Each team receives approximately eight hours of supervision and training a week, averaging about two hours per family per week. The program staff members believe that extensive supervisory time is necessary to plan for the most appropriate clinical interventions. Training is provided in structural and strategic family treatment, brief therapies, treatment of sexual abuse, chemical dependency, and family violence, in addition to training in family life education, nutrition, and the use of community resources.

Staff members are selected on the basis of their flexibility and commitment to working with multiproblem families, and for their belief in the importance of strengthening families so they can remain intact. Staff members are expected to have expertise in crisis intervention, family systems therapy, and in-home treatment, and an ability to form working relationships with other community and social service providers.

The program has developed an interagency Advisory Committee

consisting of representatives of many public and private agencies providing services to children and families within York County.

Program Design: Initial Phases

Referrals. Referrals are received from one of the four agencies making up Maine's Interdepartmental Committee for Children and Families. This committee is composed of the Departments of Corrections; Education and Cultural Services; Human Services; and Mental Health and Retardation. The committee concentrates on the coordination of services and program development for Maine's children, with an emphasis on serving families with children who are disadvantaged, handicapped, or at risk of removal from their homes.

Referrals are received at Sweetser by an administrative assistant who logs and passes them to the director of intake services and the family preservation treatment supervisor, both of whom determine the referral's appropriateness for service. When referrals exceed the program's capacity to accept new cases, the referral source is informed of the next available date for service.

Case selection. Families are eligible if their situation is serious enough for out-of-home placement to be considered were intensive services not available. The risk of placement is more broadly defined than in other family preservation programs. Many families have crises or chronic problems that often place children at risk of future, not necessarily immediate, removal. The family situation must be assessed as safe for children, parents, and program staff members. Referral sources must also concur that other community resources have been exhausted. Additionally, parents or legal guardians must indicate in writing their willingness to work with the family preservation team. In cases where a child has been recently removed from the family, the case may be considered appropriate if the child is to be returned within seven days.

Referred families primarily have school-age children. (Other community programs focus on early intervention with families with younger children.) Family problems have included sexual abuse; substance abuse; child abuse and neglect; unmanageable child behaviors and school problems; delinquency; and divorce and stepparenting difficulties. Families are described by the staff as multiproblem, many with a history of involvement with community-based and placement social service agencies.

Intake/assessment. Once a referral is determined to be appropriate, the initial interview is scheduled to take place in the family's home within one week of the initial contact with the family. During a two-week assessment period, the staff explores the family's: understanding of the problem(s); strengths and resources; patterns of communication; school and social adjustments; contacts with outside systems; and history of its critical life events. A genogram is used as an assessment tool in understanding the family's past and present dynamics. Goals for treatment are established within this two-week period.

Program Design: Service Delivery

Duration.   The program works with families for a maximum of nine weeks. This time period was selected as an appropriate compromise between the shorter four to six-week programs and Maine's home-based model, which offers a 12-week span. Staff members are available to families once services have terminated, typically for encouragement or support.

Intensity.   Teams spend one- to two-hour regularly scheduled sessions with families twice a week, at times convenient for family members. Teams spend another two to three hours a week, as needed, working with collateral resources, typically schools, social service agencies, or extended family members. The staff is available 24 hours a day and can be reached through the Sweetser switchboard operator, who in turn contacts assigned or backup personnel.

Site.   Teams work with families in their homes and communities. Staff members believe that home-based services contribute to a better understanding of the family's dynamics and environmental relationships, and also avoid the stigma often associated with service delivery within mental health or child protective service agencies.

Services.   Services are delivered with a strong clinical orientation and include in-home family therapy, family life education, advocacy and coordination with community agencies. Family visits are structured and time-limited. Staff members spend a great deal of time planning the interventions for each family situation. It is the program's philosophy that if interventions are carefully thought out, strategies are used with skill and proper timing, and community systems are appropriately involved, changes can happen quickly within the family unit. Strategic and structural family therapy theories and techniques provide the framework for service delivery.

Evaluation and Success Rates

Seventy-three percent of the children in families receiving the programs's services are in their home at the termination of service.

Funding

Sweetser's family preservation services are currently funded through a contract with the State Department of Mental Health. The funds are administered by the Department and are derived from a consortium of agencies including mental health, social services, and juvenile services.

Youth Service, Inc.
PROJECT SAFE
CRITTENTON FAMILY SUPPORT CENTER
6325 BURBRIDGE STREET
PHILADELPHIA, PENNSYLVANIA 19144
(215) 848-6200

Program History and Background

Youth Service, Inc. is a multiservice child welfare agency that provides a range of placement, in-home, and support services to children, youths, and families.

In July 1985, Youth Service, Inc. was selected by the Philadelphia Department of Human Services (DHS) to develop a joint demonstration project to provide brief, intensive, in-home services to prevent the unnecessary separation of children from their families: Project SAFE (Supportive Action for Family Empowerment).

DHS operates and contracts with many private agencies to provide an array of Services to Children in their Own Homes (SCOH). Services are categorized in three levels of intensity and offered to families in need of services to prevent the placement of children outside the family unit or to reunite children in families where placement has occurred. Services are provided on an ongoing basis, usually 12 to 18 months, and include counseling, parenting and life skills education, advocacy, and concrete supports to families. Youth Service provides Level II and Level III services. Project SAFE offers more intense and shorter-term services to families in crisis.

Administrative Structure

The project has three full-time staff members: an M.S.W. supervisor and two master's-level social workers. The supervisor/coordinator carries one case and the other two workers carry two or three families at a time. Thus six families can be seen at one time, with a capacity to serve 25 to 30 families a year. In some situations a team of two staff members may be assigned to work with a family. Services are generally provided for a 12-week period. Project SAFE is part of the Crittenton Family Support Center and is currently administratively accountable to the associate director of Youth Service.

Program Design: Initial Phase

Project SAFE is an intensive, crisis-intervention, home-based counseling and education program that focuses on family preservation to prevent children from entering placement. To be eligible for the project's services, a child must be in imminent risk of placement and the family must agree to accept services. Services are provided for approximately six to eight hours a week for eight to 12 weeks; staff members are accessible to clients seven days a week on a 24-hour basis. Services include crisis intervention, individual and family counseling, education/life skills training, and advocacy.

Referrals.   All referrals are made by social workers at DHS. They call the project supervisor, who screens the referrals to make sure that the children are in imminent risk of placement and that the family is appropriate for service. Intake appointments are scheduled as soon as possible; preferably within 48 hours. DHS retains case management responsibilities during the course of the project's work. The DHS staff is responsible for making referrals for future DHS services after the project's services terminate.

Case selection.   Families are considered appropriate for the project when they have a child or children on the verge of placement, yet the family members are committed to working with the project to deal with family problems and remain together. Many families are involved with the courts as well as DHS because of child abuse, neglect, or juvenile delinquency. Other problems include lack of adequate housing; environmental stresses; poverty; alcohol and drug abuse; truancy; psychiatric and emotional illness; parent-child conflicts; poor parenting skills; and physical illness. Families are mainly poor, with a single head of household. Over 60% of the families served are black.

Families are considered inappropriate for the project when the safety of the family members and the staff members cannot be assured—for example, when abuse or neglect is so serious that the children remain in danger after an initial investigation; or when families live in high-rise apartment projects where violence is prevalent and staff safety cannot be assured at all hours of the day or night. Consideration is given to family strengths and the probability that family problems can be resolved within a short time frame. Families with chronic problems seem to benefit more from a longer-term in-home services program.

The project has been helpful with families with the following characteristics:

The children in the family are at imminent risk of placement, as determined by the DHS worker or court.

The parent or caregiver is somewhat cooperative and motivated, but becomes easily overwhelmed and/or depressed by the problems that confront the family.

The parent or caregiver lacks the skills that are critical in dealing with the family's problems, but has the potential to acquire the skills.

The family is experiencing a current crisis rather than chronic problems.

The family has continuing housing and utility problems and frequently needs help in using community resources.

The family has had unfounded complaints of child abuse, or has had an indicated or founded complaint of child abuse that constitutes an isolated event for the family.

The family has serious relationship problems, that is, family violence or spouse abuse, which adversely affect the physical, mental, or emotional development of the child(ren).

Intake/assessment. The initial family visit is in the home and usually includes the DHS worker and the project's supervisor and staff, but this can be altered in relation to the individual family's circumstances. During the first two weeks of service, an assessment is made of the family situation, including problems, strengths, and willingness to participate intensively with the project's staff. Service needs are identified and appropriate short-term goals are established with family members.

At the end of six weeks of service, a case review meeting is held with DHS and the project's supervisors and practitioners. The family is invited to participate in this meeting, to review what goals have been met and what directions should be taken in the remaining weeks of service.

Program Design: Service Delivery

Duration.   The project serves families for up to 12 weeks. This time period was selected as necessary to meet the multiple needs of the families served. Approximately 45% of the families are referred after case closure for further services through a SCOH program, and the other 55% continue to have DHS monitoring services for three to six months.

Intensity.   Staff members spend an average of six hours a week with each family. Toward the end of the 12-week period, services are decreased somewhat to strengthen the family's autonomy.

Site.   Services take place in the family's home and community. Much advocacy and service coordination is done with other programs in the community.

Services.   The project offers a wide array of family-centered services, including counseling with the family or individual family members; client advocacy and linkages with community resources; and concrete and tangible services such as home repairs by the agency handyman, emergency food and clothing, nursing care, or purchasing beds. Life skills and parent education, housekeeping, budgeting, and respite in the Youth Service Emergency Shelter and day care program are also offered.

The staff uses a creative mix of therapeutic interventions and concrete services to engage families, build trust, help them to identify their problems, and teach new problem-solving skills. Staff members concentrate their efforts on nurturing families, building self-esteem, dealing with relationship and parenting issues, and effecting systems change. In addition, the 12-week time period is used as a guide to accomplish key tasks and to encourage independence from the staff.

Evaluation and Success

At case closing, 88% of the families who received Project SAFE services remained intact. A questionnaire has been developed to follow up families six months after closing.

Funding

Project SAFE was funded initially by the Edna McConnell Clark Foundation through the Philadelphia Department of Human Services, Children and Youth (DHS). As of July 1, 1987, DHS began contracting with Youth Service to continue Project SAFE services. Performance standards have also been developed as a part of this effort.

Appendix B—Resource Organizations

American Bar Association
1800 M Street, NW
Suite 200S
Washington, DC 20036-5886
(202) 331-2200

*American Public Welfare
Association*
810 First Street, NE
Suite 500
Washington, DC 20002
(202) 682-0100

*Center for the Study of Social
Policy*
1250 Eye Street, NW
Suite 503
Washington, DC 20005
(202) 371-1565

Children's Defense Fund
122 C Street, NW
Washington, DC 20001
(202) 628-8787

*Child Welfare League of
America*
440 First Street, NW
Suite 310
Washington, DC 20001-2085
(202) 638-2952

Florida Mental Health Institute
13301 Bruce B. Downs Blvd.
Tampa, FL 33612
(813) 974-4500

*National Association of Foster
Care Reviewers*
363 No. First Avenue
Suite A
Phoenix, AZ 85003
(602) 381-1601

*National Child Welfare Leader-
ship Center*
University of North Carolina
PO Box 3100
Chapel Hill, NC 27515-3100
(919) 966-2646

National Conference of State
Legislatures
  1050 17th Street, Suite 2100
  Denver, CO 80265
  (303) 623-7800

National Council of Juvenile
and Family Court Judges
  University of Nevada
  PO Box 8978
  Reno, NV 89507
  (702) 784-6014

National Legal Resource Center
for Child Advocacy and
Protection
  American Bar Association
  1800 M Street, NW
  Washington, DC 20036-5886
  (202) 331-2250

Youth Law Center
  1663 Mission Street
  San Francisco, CA 94103
  (415) 543-3379

Appendix C—Additional Readings

Barth, Richard P., and Berry, Marianne. "Outcomes of Child Welfare Services Under Permanency Planning." *Social Science Review* 61 (March 1987): 71–90.

Behavioral Sciences Institute. *Homebuilders Cost Effectiveness with Various Client Populations, 1974-1985.* Federal Way, WA: Behavioral Sciences Institute, 1986.

Citizens for Missouri's Children. *Where's My Home? A Study of Missouri's Children in Out-of-Home Placement.* St. Louis, MO: Citizens for Missouri's Children, 1989.

Cohen, Sheldon, and Hoberman, Harry. "Positive Events and Social Supports as Buffers of Life Change Stress." *Journal of Applied Social Psychology* 13, 2 (April 1983): 99–125.

Edna McConnell Clark Foundation. *Keeping Families Together: The Case for Family Preservation.* New York: Edna McConnell Clark Foundation, 1985.

Haygeman, J.A. *The Interpersonal Checklist: Its Use in Identifying Client Families Associated with Success or Relapse After Termination with the Homebuilders Program.* Tacoma, WA: Washington State Department of Social and Health Sciences, 1982.

Hutchinson, Janet R. *Preventive Services to Families in Four States: Subcontractor's Final Report.* Iowa City, IA: The National Resource Center on Family-Based Services, School of Social Work, University of Iowa, 1987.

Hutchinson, Janet, and Borah, Kathleen. *A Comparative Analysis of the Costs of Substitute Care and Family Based Services.* Iowa City, IA:

The National Resource Center on Family-Based Services, School of Social Work, University of Iowa, 1982.

Jones, M.; Magura, S.; and Shyne, A., "Effective Practice with Families in Protective and Preventative Services: What Works?" *Child Welfare* LX, 2 (February 1981): 66–79.

Jones, M.A. *A Second Chance for Families: Five Years Later.* New York: Child Welfare League of America, 1985.

Knitzer, J., and Cole, E. *Family Preservation Services: The Program Challenge for Child Welfare and Child Mental Health Agencies.* New York: Changing Services for Children, Bank Street College of Education, 1989.

Lahti, J.; Green, K.; Emlen, K.; Zadny, J.; Clarkson, Q.D.; and Kuchnel Casciato, J. *A Follow-Up Study of the Oregon Project.* Portland, OR: Portland State University, Regional Institute for Human Services, 1978.

Landsman, Miriam T. *Evaluation of Fourteen Child Placement Prevention Projects in Wisconsin 1983–1985.* Iowa City, IA: The National Resource Center on Family-Based Services, 1985.

Leitenberg, Harold; Burchard, J.; Healy, D.; and Fuller, E.J. "Non-Delinquent Children in State Custody: Does Type of Placement Matter?" *American Journal of Community Psychology* 9 (June 1981): 347–360.

Lyle, Charles G., and Nelson, John. *Home Based vs. Traditional Child Protection Services: A Study of the Home Based Services Demonstration Project in the Ramsey County Community Human Services Department.* Unpublished manuscript, Ramsey County Community Human Services, Minnesota, July 27, 1983.

Magura, S. "Are Services to Prevent Foster Care Effective?" *Children and Youth Service Review* 3 (n.d.): 193–212.

Magura, S., and DeRubeis, R. *The Effectiveness of Preventive Services for Families with Abused, Neglected and Disturbed Children: Second Year Evaluation of the Hudson County Project.* Trenton, NJ: Division of Youth and Family Services, Bureau of Research, n.d.

Magura, S.; Moses, B.; and Jones, M. *Assessing and Measuring Change in Families.* Washington, DC: Child Welfare League of America, 1987.

Milardo, Robert. "Social Networks and Pair Relationships: A Review of Substantive and Measurement Issues." *Sociology and Social Research* 68 (1983): 1–18.

Pecora, P.J., et al. *Defining Family Preservation Services: Three Intensive Home-Based Treatment Programs.* Salt Lake City, UT: Research Report Number 1 from the Family-Based Intensive Treatment Project, University of Utah, Graduate School of Social Work, Social Research Institute, 1987.

Reidy, Thomas. "The Aggressive Characteristics of Abused and Neglected Children." *Journal of Clinical Psychology* 33 (October 1977): 1140–1145.

Stein, T.J. "Projects to Prevent Out-of-Home Placements." *Children and Youth Services Review* 7 (January/February 1985): 109–122.

Wald, Michael S., et al. *Protecting Abused and Neglected Children: A Comparison of Home and Foster Placements.* Stanford, CA: Stanford University Center for the Study of Youth Development, 1985.

Webb, Eugene J.; Campbell, Donald T.; Schwartz, Richard D.; and Sechrest, Lee. *Unobtrusive Measures: Nonreactive Research in the Social Sciences.* Chicago, IL: Rand McNally, 1986.

Yuan, Ying-Ying T., and Rivest, Michele. *Evaluation Resources for Family Preservation Services.* Washington, DC: Center for the Support of Children, 1988.

About the Authors

Elizabeth S. (Betsy) Cole, M.S.W., is President of Elizabeth S. Cole Associates, New Hope, Pennsylvania, a consulting firm specializing in children's services. In this capacity, Ms. Cole acts as advisor and consultant to national organizations such as the National Conference of Juvenile and Family Court Judges, the National Child Welfare Leadership Center, and the National Resource Center on Special Needs Adoption.

Ms. Cole's work experience includes 15 years in the New Jersey public child welfare system as caseworker, supervisor, and bureau chief. As former Director of the North American Center on Adoption and former Director of Permanent Families for Children at the Child Welfare League of America, Ms. Cole has done training, speaking, and consultation across the United States and in Canada, Great Britain, Australia, and South Africa.

Ms. Cole is the author of a number of written works on such child welfare topics as family preservation, permanency planning, and adoption. She received her Master of Social Work from Rutgers University.

Joy Duva, M.S.W., is Director of Professional Services for Casey Family Services, Shelton, Connecticut. From July 1987 to August 1989, Ms. Duva directed Family Preservation Services for the Child Welfare League of America, Washington, D.C.

Ms. Duva is the former Director of Child Welfare for the State of Maryland, and was responsible for developing family preservation services in the state. Prior to that, she served as Resource Director for the Military Family Resource Center. She received her Master of Social Work from Fordham University.